This series offers the concerned reader basic guidelines and *practical* applications of religion for today's world. Although decidedly Christian in focus and emphasis, the series embraces all denominations and modes of Bible-based belief relevant to our lives today. All volumes in the Steeple series are originals, freshly written to provide a fresh perspective on current—and yet timeless—human dilemmas. This is a series for our times. Among the books:

How to Read the Bible
James Fischer

Soulwinning: An Action Handbook for Christians
Reg A. Forder

A Spiritual Handbook for Women
Dandi Daley Knorr

Temptation: How Christians Can Deal with It
Frances Carroll

*With God on Your Side: A Guide to Finding
Self-Worth Through Total Faith*
Doug Manning

*A Daily Key for Today's Christians:
365 Key Texts of the New Testament*
William E. Bowles

*Eight Stages of Christian Growth:
Human Development in Psycho-Spiritual Terms*
Philip A. Captain/foreword by Jerry Falwell

How to Pray: Discovering New Spiritual Growth Through Prayer
Barbara A. Gawle

Frustration: How Christians Can Deal with It
Frances Carroll

*How to Talk with God Every Day of the Year:
A Book of Devotions for Twelve Positive Months*
Frances Hunter

*God's Conditions for Prosperity:
How to Earn the Rewards of Christian Living*
Charles Hunter

*A Child of God: Activities for Teaching Spiritual Values
to Children of All Ages*
Peggy D. Jenkins

Prentice-Hall International (UK) Limited, *London*
Prentice-Hall of Australia Pty. Limited, *Sydney*
Prentice-Hall Canada Inc., *Toronto*
Prentice-Hall Hispanoamericana, S.A., *Mexico*
Prentice-Hall of India Private Limited, *New Delhi*
Prentice-Hall of Japan, Inc., *Tokyo*
Prentice-Hall of Southeast Asia Pte. Ltd., *Singapore*
Whitehall Books Limited, *Wellington, New Zealand*
Editora Prentice-Hall do Brasil Ltda., *Rio de Janeiro*

Frances Loftiss Carroll

How to Talk with Your Children About God

A SPECTRUM BOOK

Prentice-Hall, Inc., Englewood Cliffs, New Jersey 07632

Library of Congress Cataloging in Publication Data

Carroll, Frances L.
  How to talk with your children about God.

  (Steeple books)
  "A Spectrum Book."
  Includes index.
  1. Children—Religious life.   2. Christian
  education of children.   I. Title.   II. Series.
  BV4571.2.C375   1985   248.8′4   84-22293
  ISBN 0-13-435207-6
  ISBN 0-13-435199-1 (pbk.)

11-85

1   2   3   4   5   6   7   8   9   10

ISBN 0-13-435207-6

ISBN 0-13-435199-1 {PBK.}

Editorial/production supervision by Lauren DeLuca
Cover design by Hal Siegel
Manufacturing buyer: Frank Grieco

Scripture quotations marked (NIV) are from the Holy Bible,
New International Version. Copyright 1973, 1978,
International Bible Society. Scripture quotations marked (NKJV)
are from the New King James Version. Copyright © 1979, 1980, 1982,
Thomas Nelson, Inc., Publishers. Scripture quotations marked (NAS)
are from the New American Standard Bible, © The Lockman
Foundation 1960, 1962, 1963, 1968, 1971, 1972, 1973, 1975, 1977.
Reprinted by permission of the Lockman Foundation. Scripture
quotations marked (Williams) are from the Williams New Testament
by Charles B. Williams, Copyright 1937, 1965, 1966 by Edith Williams.
Used by permission of Moody Press, Moody Bible Institute of Chicago.

This book is dedicated, with love, to these people:

David Miller, associate pastor and brother in Christ, First Baptist Church, Russellville, Arkansas. My brother David has been more than my pastor friend. He has taken upon himself some of my burdens, displayed Christ-like love, shown me that the Lord has challenges for those who are His, and been an unwavering Christian friend. David's life genuinely reflects Christ's commandment to "Love one another as I have loved you."

Mary Kennan, editor, for her dedication and commitment to a belief she holds deeply in her heart. Mary has believed in this project from day one. She is more than my editor; she is my friend.

Norma Ledbetter, formerly of Prentice-Hall's General Publishing Division, who time and time again told me, "You've got what it takes"—for sharing her knowledge, her sense of humor, and her love with a writer who had no idea what was going on.

Contents

chapter one
Introduction to Parents, 1

chapter two
God, 7

chapter three
The Trinity, 35

chapter four
Jesus Christ, the Son of God, 43

chapter five
Jesus' Gift, 61

chapter six
Accepting Jesus' Gift, 77

chapter seven
The Holy Spirit, 91

chapter eight
Gifts and Talents, 101

chapter nine
The Importance of Prayer, 109

chapter ten
Growing in Faith and in Love, 123

chapter eleven
Questions of Interest to Children, 133

Appendix, 141

Index, 151

Preface

Children are a precious gift from God. Our lives are truly blessed by their presence in our homes. The Christian parent who holds a tiny infant in his or her arms feels joy and awe. We thank God for allowing the child to be a part of our family, and we dedicate our efforts to giving the child a good life.

As we watch our children grow, many thoughts enter our minds. We want the best for them, and that best includes a personal relationship with God. As we pray for guidance and ask God to show us how to train our children concerning the values of life, there is often a feeling of inadequacy. Many of us find that we are not really prepared to share our faith with our children, but what are we to do?

It is my hope that this book will address the questions and supply the answers you need to discuss God with your children. I have searched the Scriptures and prayed for guidance through the Holy Spirit throughout this entire project. My ultimate authority is the Holy Bible, the Word of God. My thoughts and ideas are based on my personal efforts to learn new truths from God, and I pray that they are guided by the wisdom of the Holy Spirit. In this book I have tried to focus on the basic Christian philosophy concerning life as presented in the Bible. The book is not intended to present the view of any particular denomination.

This book should be helpful to anyone who reads it. It will supply guidance, self-help, encouragement, and an outpouring of Christian love to the reader. It is intended to help you lead your child to the full knowledge of God the Father, God the Son, and God the Holy Spirit. Through your study and application your children should view God and His Son—our Lord Jesus Christ—in a more personal manner. I think it will help them understand more of the Christian faith and what God's plan for their life might be. It is my prayer that God will allow this book to become an effective tool in His work and that He will be glorified through it.

How to
Talk with Your
Children
About God

chapter one

Introduction to Parents

All Christian parents want their children to know about God. It is our desire that they gain knowledge of God; and yet where do we turn to gain information about God? As concerned parents, we must determine what concepts to teach our children about the Christian life. For some of us the task is simple. For others it is seemingly impossible.

A balance is needed in discussing God with our children. We need to share our spiritual enthusiasm and yet not to become too zestful as we share our faith. Our task is to plant seeds of faith and watch as God allows them to grow. Our greatest task is to be genuine, to be authentic as we talk about God. We shouldn't allow ourselves to get "uptight" or become embarrassed when we share our beliefs with our children. They understand that parents really don't have all the answers. They know we aren't anywhere near perfect. When our children perceive our faith as strong and real, we need not be needlessly concerned about how to discuss our faith.

There is no reason to be perplexed concerning opportunities to share God because children, from the beginning of their lives, feel trust and love. As you cared for your baby and talked with him or or her, a bond of love has developed and grown between you. In sharing your faith, be confident in this bond. You are the child's strongest influence and his or her protector. A strong bond of love exists between you and the child with whom you are sharing God. Carry the thought in your heart that this boy or girl is interested in learning about God. As they see you exercise your trust in Christ and allow His Spirit to work through you, then they will desire to know more about the Christian way of life.

You are an example—good, bad, or indifferent—to your boy or girl. You can make the difference in your child's response to God's call. Your attitude toward Christ is not to be underestimated. Your children are more receptive to the love of God because they admire your faith and want to be like you. Where, then, do we begin? What is it that your child knows and understands about God, Christ, angels, heaven, hell?

Appendix A provides charts related to what your children can understand about God at different age levels. Take time now to study the charts and refer to them often. They will give you a special insight concerning what children believe and the things they understand in relationship to God. I think it will be most helpful to you as you begin to discuss God with your children.

Teaching the Child in the Home

As parents, we are responsible for building the foundation for our children's faith. Faith and believing begin first within the home. Although Sunday School and church attendance are encouraged and necessary for balanced spiritual growth, parents must maintain full responsibility to talk about God and encourage religious training.

From the first moment your child begins to toddle around the house and communications begin, it is important to share God.

For example, while showing your toddler a leaf or a pretty flower you might say something like, "Isn't that a pretty flower? Wasn't it nice for God to put it here for us to share?" Although you may not consider this simple statement important, the child has received some valuable exposure to God. You have introduced him or her to God and nature at the same time. A beginning has been made, with almost no effort. You have planted a seed of faith. It is really enjoyable to talk to children about God. Most of them are quite curious and very receptive to the love God has to offer them.

Opportunities are ever present to talk to your children about God, especially His beautiful nature. For example, as our family wandered along a path at the Petit Jean State Park near Morrilton, Arkansas, I found a natural opportunity to share with our two children. Ray (age 9) was running his fingers through the waters of a tiny stream. Mary Ann (age 11) was collecting autumn leaves. My husband, Sandy, was scouting around for something unusual to share with the kids and I was leaning on a rock resting. "Kids, wasn't it nice of God to make such a beautiful place for us to have a nature hike?" I said cheerfully.

"Sure was, Mom," replied Ray. "Did you notice how pretty all the rocks are as the water runs over them?" he said, splashing his fingers through the water.

Mary Ann responded, "God sure made some beautiful leaves too. Look at these, Mom."

See how simple it was to introduce God into our nature hike? Too often we overlook those precious moments. In fact, God was mentioned by the children several times that day. As we journeyed onward to the Bear Caves and walked over the naturally sculptured turtle rocks, Ray said, "God even made some things funny, didn't He?" We all laughed as we considered God having a sense of humor.

Mary Ann stated at Cedar Falls, "I think God put the falls in just the right spot." As we watched the waters tumble over the edge of the cliff and fall into the pool below, Mary Ann spoke, "I'm so sure that God planned to put the falls here. I think He chose the perfect place. He knew that a lot of people would come here just to visit this beautiful waterfall." Mary Ann was reaffirming her belief in God creating earth as well as expressing her feelings.

My point is that you can enjoy sharing God everywhere. In fact, I consider the zoo a natural place to discuss God's creativity. In nature, there is always something unique and individual. Not to mention the fact that within the realm of even the smallest zoo there are some strange creatures. Zoos are fun! Zoos are educational and most of all zoos provide special opportunities to share some beliefs about God creating each animal and the universe.

Another fantastic way to discover the beauty of God is to look for rocks. Rocks come in all sizes, shapes, textures, and colors. Our family is a bunch of rockhounds—we enjoy looking at and for rocks. Rocks are a natural wonder. It's fun to hold them in your hand and examine them closely. When you locate some agates in a stream, notice how they shine. Surely God took some special effort to color these simple little stones. Our God is a special, loving, concerned Father who encourages us to enjoy the beauty of the earth as He created it.

You would be delightfully surprised at the frequency with which our children mention something about God as we search for our "special rocks." You see, we don't need a designated time or a certain atmosphere to discuss God; opportunities are ever present. When children learn from early childhood that God is a significant part of life they will want to share God at every opportunity.

There is no reason to fret about talking with your children about God. It simply takes a little time and some loving effort. To a child, it seems, everything they are involved in is important. We only need to set a time and plant seeds for God's Word to become real and certain. As the Word grows and blooms, then we will experience unspoken happiness as our children learn to love and accept God's gift of new life for them, through Jesus Christ. As we develop the habit of being sensitive to the needs of our children and become actively involved in their lives, God will provide the chances to share His Word in a special manner. Each Christian parent should help their boy or girl find God by providing a loving atmosphere and a happy home.

Providing a Bible for your young person is also important. What translation should you use with your child? There are many translations available and I would like to suggest two of them:

1. The New International Version
2. The Living Bible

Also, I find the Williams New Testamanet, the Phillips New Testament, and the Good News Bible good as alternate versions. The need is to understand the Word of God, apply it to your heart and then to use it in your daily life. Isn't that true? Well, to make these things happen we must first understand what we are reading. There is time to move up to a deeper translation such as the King James, New King James, or the New American Standard at a later date. Your children will let you know when they are ready to learn more and then you can change to another version, and they are on their way.

It is important to share God in your home through a special love relationship with each member of the family. How you respond to life and God determines, in part, the acceptance your own children will have to God. If God is personal to you then more than likely He will become personal to your children. Don't think that because you are a Christian your children will be too. This isn't necessarily true! Children need to be guided to God in a loving and sensitive manner. If you aren't involved in that opportunity then make a decision to become involved.

The greatest joy Christian parents can experience is to know that our children have found the Lord and known Him in a personal manner. What more could we ask than that our precious children belong to the family of God?

The challenge is before us. It is not as impossible as it seems. As we discuss faith with our children the Holy Spirit will work through us and teach them at their own pace. He knows what they need to hear in order to respond to Him. Who better than you and I can share the love of God with our own children? The answer is certain—*no one*! As parents we are to be instruments, tools for the Living God. We must allow God to teach us too so that we might wisely discuss the love of God with His most precious gift to us, our children. We are to pray, study, listen and learn from the Scriptures as taught through the wisdom of the Holy Spirit, who lives within the heart of each Christian.

In studying the various topics we will:

1. Supply the question or topic.
2. Answer briefly for adult consideration.
3. Present scripture passages where appropriate.
4. Answer for the child at their level of understanding.
5. Provide discussion and ideas beyond answers to questions.

Remember, it is up to the parent to dig deeper into the Word of God. It should be your personal goal to know more about the scriptures today than you knew yesterday.

Not all the questions in this study are fully explained. Some of them need your personal input and investigation so that you might more fully explore the Bible on your own.

Let us begin, now!

chapter two

God

As we discuss God with our children we rediscover the value of reading the Bible as individuals as well as families. There is an immense amount of information to absorb concerning God and none of us ever know all the answers to the countless questions concerning God. Sometimes parents become concerned about answering their children's questions adequately. While this may cause some concerns, children really do understand when parents say, "I don't know the answer," or "I am not sure." We are, after all, only human.

One of our greatest opportunities to share God is through Bible story books and reading stories from the Scriptures. Recall your own childhood. Weren't stories such as Samson and Delilah, David and Goliath, and Jesus and the feeding of the multitudes exciting? They still are! Your boy or girl is as anxious as you were to hear these great stories.

So then, having laid a foundation of our needs and responses to our children we must ask ourselves—"How do I tell my children about God?" The answer is found in sharing on a daily basis. Let's begin by asking a few questions about God and rediscovering the answers. To simplify our study we will ask questions and then use Scriptures as guidance for our answers.

It is my wish to encourage the reader to read and study the Holy Bible independently. Answering children with the simplest answer may be best but you, as a parent, need more answers to gain deeper understanding of God's plan for life. It is my hope this plan will expand your spiritual insight and you will become a more knowledgeable Christian.

In the areas where I have commented, I have made it clear that it is my opinion. It is not my desire to add to or detract from the Word of God but merely to provide additional thoughts for discussion and to stimulate your thinking?

Where did God come from?

To the Adult. I can almost see you cringe. Every human being desires the answer to this pertinent question. Who among us has not faced an embarrassed adult who confesses, "I don't know!" This is the perfect moment to reiterate that there are many things for which there is no clear answer. God has not revealed everything of importance to us. If we were as intelligent as God, would we need Him? More than likely we would not! If we held the key to unlock all of the mysteries of the world, few people, if any, would seek to know God in a personal manner.

Okay, now let's ponder this question. I expect you would like a complete answer, wouldn't you? Well, it's just not that simple, for God is unexplainable. Our finite minds cannot fully comprehend the infinite God. It is at this point our faith springs into action. Faith is hearing, considering, and accepting biblical facts. God is, and was in the beginning and will continue to be *forever more.* As we give our trust to God and believe the Bible our faith is allowed to function as God intends it to.

Bear in mind that as we allow our faith to work God knows all and our knowledge is limited. Some questions studied here can only be answered by God. As we discuss God with our children we must know that their reasoning and understanding are not the same as an adult's. When our answers are simply stated, children are usually satisfied.

I have supplied Scriptures for use as reference material. You may or may not want to use them as you discuss God with your children. I may respond to some questions as though I was speaking with our children, Mary Ann and Ray Jr. Perhaps the answers will be of interest to you and you will incorporate them in your discussions with your children. Other questions will be answered directly.

Let's open our Bible and read some verses which help us to understand God a little better. (Remember we are speaking to children. Speak in terms they will understand.)

To the Child. First, *I don't know!* Second, no one knows. Nor do we know how long He has been here. You see, Ray, there are simply some things God keeps as His secrets.

God will supply the answers to all of our questions, someday, when we are together with Him in heaven. I doubt that we could understand all of God's mysteries if He told them to us, anyway. Some things are impossible for humans to understand because we think of time as today and tomorrow. With God all time is eternal (forever) and God knows humans have a difficult time thinking too far ahead. The most important thing to remember, Ray, is God doesn't consider this question serious enough to give us the answer now. What God does consider important is that we know He loves us and cares for us.

"God is spirit, and his worshippers must worship in spirit and in truth." John 4:24 (NIV)

" 'You are My witnesses,' says the Lord, 'And My servant whom I have chosen, That you may know and believe Me, And understand that I am He. Before Me there was no God formed, Nor shall there be after Me. I, even, I am the LORD, And besides Me there is no savior. I have declared and saved, I have proclaimed, And there was no foreign god among you; Therefore you are My

9

witnesses,' Says the LORD, 'that I am God. Indeed before the day was, I am He; And there is no one who can deliver out of My hand; I work, and who will reverse it?' " Isaiah 43:10-13 (NKJV)

"Thus says the LORD, the King of Israel, And his Redeemer, the LORD of hosts: 'I am the First and I am the Last; Besides Me there is no God.' " Isaiah 44:6 (NKJV)

"For thus says the LORD,
Who created the heavens,
Who is GOD,
Who formed the earth and made it,
Who established it,
Who did not create it in vain,
Who formed it to be inhabited:
'I AM the LORD, and there is no other.' "
    Isaiah 45:18 (NKJV)

Additional Discussion

As you can see from the Scriptures, we have some difficult thoughts to deal with but we will not allow the weight of the words to become burdensome. The Holy Spirit will reveal new insights to us as we study and apply the Word of God.

Within our Scripture texts we have a variety of information given us about God. Let's review the question and then consider the information on which we have to draw a conclusion and supply an answer.

In the above passages, we have studied information about God. Here is what we have learned.

- God is a spirit.
- God is the First and the Last.
- Besides God there is no other god.

- God is the creator, the one who was in the beginning.
- God is also the one who makes life possible.

We know that the secrets of the universe are yet locked within God's teasure chest. There are some things we know for certain:

1. God always was and still is.
2. Only God knows the mystery of His origin.
3. God formed all life and the unverse.
4. God is all wisdom and knowledge.
5. There is only one God and none other.

In discussing God with our children there are some things we must make clear from the beginning. First, God reveals to us the things He wants us to know. Had God wanted us to know more about Him and where He came from we would have been supplied this information. You see, we have yet to understand the hidden secrets of the universe. They are not nearly as complicated and complex as the Spirit of God. In this century, mankind has sought to discover the secrets of life. Space travel, electricity, air travel, computers, automobiles, television and so many more discoveries of the 20th century have yet to be totally explored. How can we expect to understand God until we first know about ourselves?

Secondly, God is almighty and powerful, the One who knows and sees all. How He can do this is not known by us. The important truth of this statement is that we should believe, accept, and appreciate God. Surely, the same God who watched over Adam, Eve, Moses, Noah, Joshua, David, Job, Paul, John, Peter, and all those who have lived before us, knows us. We should cherish the fact that we are of concern to Him. We should know too that God desires that our spirits communicate with Him. He created us to experience an in-depth relationship with Him. We will discuss this idea later on.

Thirdly, in understanding God's origin the answer for a child is simple: it *really* doesn't matter. The important thing to recall is that *He still is*, and *God does care for you and me*. He wants us to know Him in a special way, as His adopted children. To know Him, we must learn about Him through His Word, and Holy Bible. We then must desire to have God as a part of our life. We will want to discover that God is love and He wants to give those who love Him a life filled with the treasures of God.

With the information and discussion of this first question, you should now have a good idea what you want to relate to your child concerning God. Most of the information is easily related to children. It really isn't difficult, is it? Most of our answers are unnecessarily complicated aren't they? Be truthful and state your ideas in simple terms. Of course, *always* pray before you speak of these precious truths so that the Holy Spirit might encourage and guide your spirit.

Who is God?

Remember that these are young people with whom we are discussing God, not a theologian.

To the Adult. This question makes us wonder when the easy questions are going to come up, doesn't it? Well, it is a difficult but not impossible question to answer. The greatest obstacle for us to overcome in answering these questions may be our own feelings of inadequacy. We aren't sure what to answer, are we? Well, it is my hope these Scripture passages will help us understand a bit better ourselves as well as help our children to understand.

"Ask now about the former days, long before your time, from the day God created man on earth; ask from one end of the heavens to the other. Has anything so great as this ever happened, or has anything like it ever been heard of? Have any other people heard the voice of God speaking out of fire, as you have, and lived? Has any god ever tried to take for himself one nation out of another nation, by testings, by miraculous signs and wonders, by war, by a mighty hand and an outstretched arm, or by great and

awesome deeds, like all the things the LORD your God did for you in Egypt before your very eyes? You were shown these things so that you might know that the LORD is God; besides him there is no other." Deuteronomy 4:32-35 (NIV)

"Rather, worship the LORD your God; it is he who will deliver you from the hand of all your enemies." 2 Kings 17:39 (NIV)

"And said: O LORD, God of Israel, there is no God like you in heaven above or on earth below—you who keep your covenant of love with your servants who continue wholeheartedly in your way." 1 Kings 8:23 (NIV)

"And this is the message that we have heard from Him and now announce to you: God is light, and there is no darkness at all in Him." 1 John 1:5 (Williams)

"For God is greater than our hearts, and he knows everything." 1 John 3:20b (NIV)

"And we have seen and testify that the Father has sent his Son to be the Savior of the world. If anyone acknowledges that Jesus is the Son of God, God lives in him and he in God. And so we know and rely on the love God has for us. God is love. Whoever lives in love lives in God, and God in him." 1 John 4:14-16 (NIV)

"And God said to Moses, "I AM WHO I AM." And He said, "Thus you shall say to the children of Israel, I AM has sent me to you." Exodus 3:14 (NKJV)

To the Child. God is the one who created all things. He is the one we should worship and pray to for all our needs. There is no god but our God.

Additional Discussion

I expect the Scriptures referenced above tend to put you at ease about who God is and how to relate this to your children. This question, not quite as complex as the last, gives more information to use in relating God to our young person.

Let's review some of the insight we have gained in these Scriptures.

- God said to Moses, "I AM WHO I AM."

The voice of authority, God spoke to Moses and reassured him that He (God) was the ultimate and supreme authority. He was the one and only true God. No doubt Moses was fearful. Here he stood, in the presence of God, trembling and wondering why God has chosen to give him this message. Moses knew, without any doubt, that God was what He stated, "I AM." Moses learned first-hand not to question God but do what God commanded. Never again did he question the authority of God.

- 1 John 3:20 allows us to see that God is greatest of all.

God wants us to understand that He does, indeed, know everything about us. He knows each of us intimately and personally. The greatness of God is limitless. Our knowledge is limited. This Scripture should allow us to acknowledge that the Lord God is the Supreme Being. The One who created all!

- 1 John 1:5 is meaningful in that it allows us to understand God in the terms of light and darkness.

Evil, spiritual darkness, the adversary's works of greed, hate, selfishness and sinfulness are spoken of as darkness. God is light. Light gives power, illuminates all things, and reveals flaws so that we might see things as they are. It removes shadows which allow certain unspiritual things to be seen as falsehoods and deceitful attitudes.

It is well to recall that God's works and deeds are displayed openly, in the light, for all to examine. The works of Satan often remain hidden away. They are tucked away in dark corners and not noticed by us until we become entangled in Satan's snare.

Simply stated God is the one who supplies spiritual light. Satan is the one who deceives. We must understand this simple truth and allow our youngsters to realize that God's spirit is filled with beauty and constructiveness while Satan's spirit is self-directed and destructive. Since we are seeking to discuss God in terms which will be easily understood, the above discussion should serve the purpose of helping youngsters understand that God is the giver of good. Recall, in our efforts to share God we must avoid long theological discussions which will confuse children. Remember, simplicity is best! Ours is to direct children to thinking about God by sowing seeds of faith. God does the rest.

- 1 John 4:14-16 contains two beautiful verses of Scripture.

Reread these verses. *God is love.* Where would we be without love? Everyone understands the need for love. There is a universal need for love. No matter what your heritage, American, Spanish, Italian, Canadian, British, Israelite, African, Arabian, Egyptian, Russian or a multitude of others; each heart has an inward desire to experience love. Love encompasses all of mankind, even though we often conceal it. We all crave the warmth and emotional fulfillment that God's love gives to mankind. God's love was ultimately revealed to mankind in the person of Jesus Christ. God sent His Son, the perfect representative of love, to this world so that we might know God in a more understandable manner.

Secondly, whoever lives in love lives where? In God. And where is God? In the Christian. You see, it is impossible for anyone who has been touched by or experienced the love of God not to share the genuine love of God. God's love, manifested through Jesus Christ, is ours for receiving and sharing with others. God wants us to experience love throughout each moment we live. God's love cannot be stolen away or fade away nor can it be selfishly kept to one's self. God's love is to be offered to others through us in order that we will all desire a personal relationship with Him.

Love is difficult to reject. While some people do willingly choose to reject God's love there is still an unfulfilled need for acceptance in their hearts. Those who reject God time and time again will harden their hearts and spirits toward God. Their spirits are not filled with the peace and joy which comes from God. Their motives are turned toward pleasing themselves and ignoring God. The person who continually and willingly rejects the love of God has made a firm decision as to whom and what to follow. You see, the Scriptures clearly tell us there are but two ways to go:

1. To follow God and know Jesus as Lord and Savior.
2. To follow the way of evil. That's sin.

Summary

Who then is God? Surely our examination of the Scriptures has allowed us to determine the truth. God is the beauty of all nature, the Lord of all, the ultimate expression of Love, the God of Israel. God is light. He is the creator of all. God has stated, "I am who I am." To grasp this truth and allow God to reveal it to your youngster the answer is best expressed by explaining that God is personal to us. It matters very little to a young person what others say about God, in these young years, but it is vital that they understand your convictions. Ask yourself who you believe God to be. As you consider the question allow the Spirit of God to speak to your heart and then make your own evaluation. As you do this, then, you will be prepared when you are asked, "Just who do you believe God to be?"

How can God be everywhere?

To the Adult. We are able to say that God is a spirit for we have discussed this in questions one and two. God's Spirit can be anywhere and everywhere.

Recall that we have talked about mysteries. This is another mystery to those who have trouble comprehending God. Thoughts become entangled by simple truths. We want visible proof instead of believing the Scriptures; our human nature challenges God. We need to allow our children to understand that like faith, which is also unseen, so then is God. Faith grows by allowing God to become a reality in our lives.

The phrases omnipresent and omniscient are words used to describe God, the words which mean He is always there and always has been. There are numerous Scriptures which instruct us concerning God's presence. Instead of conducting an in-depth study of these verses at this point, allow me to share a series of thoughts with you.

- Don't dazzle and amaze children by using an overload of Scripture verses.

That is to say, "Don't drown them in the Word of God." Some things we know by exposure, and children like to hear about personal experiences.

- Share moments when you know God has been near.

Where were you when you needed God most and He responded? What experiences have you or someone who is close to you had when you knew God was present and "real"?

- Be practical.

Don't be "super spiritual." Be real! You and I have experienced persons who "overwhelm" us with their attitudes and ideas concerning their "experience." While it is unintentional, these persons tend to turn us away from God. Their faith does not relate to what we know and feel. Beliefs and standards are blown out of proportion. We must regard the simplicity of faith as an individual matter. Those of us who believe in the Lord Jesus Christ are to maintain a humble attitude and a spiritual humility toward our

17

relationship with God. In other words there is no need to toot your horn. False faith or over-zealous reactions give root to shallow experiences. Even the youngest child can detect fake faith in those who profess to have all the answers. Recall that you and I are living, breathing examples of faith. What we project to another person is either genuine or unreal. Be real! Allow your young persons to see that you feel the presence of God. Share God in your heart and from your heart.

- Ask your children questions.

(My example): "Mary Ann, can you remember a time when you thought God was nearby? Did you know that God is with you all the time? Can you feel God's presence as you look at the clouds, the leaves changing color, or when you see a baby kitten?" Think about all the places that we know God has been. We need only apply our minds and rediscover God for ourselves to understand the ever presence of God.

To the Child. God has mysteries (child's name). God's Spirit can be everywhere because He has said He can do anything and be anywhere. God's Spirit is like the wind. We don't know where it comes from or where it goes but we can feel and know its presence.

How can you describe God?

To the Adult. I don't know who will enjoy this thought more: the parent or the young person. This is going to be a fun answer! There are a variety of answers which will arise as you discuss God in an open manner. Question (to your child): "Mary Ann, how would you describe God to one of your friends? What words best describe what you think God to be?" God is many things to many people. He has told us about Himself in Psalms 121. Let's open our Bible and see what God has said.

Here is a series of thoughts you might want to share about God.

"The eternal God is your refuge." Deuteronomy 33:27a (NKJV)

"To you it was shown, that you might know that the LORD Himself is God; there is none other beside Him." Deuteronomy 4:35 (NKJV)

"For I am the LORD your God, the Holy One of Israel, your Savior." Isaiah 43:3a, b, c (NKJB)

"Fear not, for I am with you; Be not dismayed, for I am your God. I will strengthen you, Yes, I will help you, I will uphold you with My righteous right hand." Isaiah 41:10 (NKJV)

"I lift up my eyes to the hills—where does my help come from? My help comes from the LORD, the Maker of heaven and earth. He will not let your foot slip—he who watches over you will not slumber; indeed he who watches over Israel will neither slumber nor sleep. The LORD watches over you—the LORD is your shade at your right hand; the sun will not harm you by day, nor the moon by night. The LORD will keep you from all harm— he will watch over your life; the LORD will watch over your coming and going both now and forevermore." Psalms 121:1-8 (NIV)

To the Child. Well now, need we say more? Read the above verses with your children. Psalms 121 sets the record straight for us in language that even a young child can understand, doesn't it? We learn how to describe God. Perhaps the simplicity of this Psalm is your answer in speaking of God. How beautiful are the Psalms and how glorious it is to discover God through the words of David. Frankly, there is little to be added to David's words.

Tell me something about God's nature.

To the Adult and Child. This question has many answers. Explore some of them through sharing these verses with your children.

"I call on the LORD in my distress, and he answers me."
"He will punish you with a warrior's sharp arrows, with burning coals of the broom tree." Psalms 120:1,4 (NIV)

"God is mightly, but does not despise men; he is mighty, and firm in his purpose." Job 36:5 (NIV)

"For the eyes of the LORD range throughout the earth to strengthen those whose hearts are fully committed to him." 2 Chronicles 16:9 (NIV)

"For the LORD your God is God of gods and Lord of lords, the great God, mighty and awesome, who shows no partiality and accepts no bribes." Deuteronomy 10:17 (NIV)

"Your arm is endued with power; your hand is strong, your right hand exalted. Righteousness and justice are the foundation of your throne; love and faithfulness go before you." Pslams 89:13,14 (NIV)

"You show love to thousands but bring the punishment for the fathers' sins into the laps of their children after them. O great and powerful God, whose name is the LORD Almighty, great are your purposes and mighty are your deeds. Your eyes are open to all the ways of men; you reward everyone according to his conduct and as his deeds deserve." Jeremiah 32:18,19 (NIV)

Additional Discussion

All of the Scriptures point to the fact that God is just, all powerful, impartial, forgiving, and mindful of us. We are of importance to God. He wants each of us to examine our hearts and determine our relationship with Him. God will not allow those who continually sin to go unpunished. They must receive the judgment of God for their deeds. While we speak openly of justice and judgment, be careful not to cause children to overreact to God's punishment of wrongdoers.

As children gain some comprehension of God's justice they should know that God does not punish those who are not in need of punishment. God wants to love and reward those who do right. He desires to shower us with blessings from His storehouse of treasures. God wants to be kind to all of us. Yet if we continually fail to do right then we must expect punishment. Children can comprehend punishment within their own family as discipline. So it is with God. We are members of God's Family. He must lovingly punish wrong to those who willfully and continually disobey Him.

God as Creator

To the Adult. To understand God as creator we must first acknowledge that He is the builder, planner, and supplier of the universe. Don't think God didn't take time to consider His creations, He did, and His efforts are majestic and beautiful. Teach your child to be thankful concerning God's handywork.

"In the beginning God created the heavens and the earth." Genesis 1:1a (NIV)

"So God created man in his own image, in the image of God he created him; male and female he created them." Genesis 1:27 (NIV)

"God saw all that he had made, and it was very good." Genesis 1:31a (NIV)

"Rich and poor have this in common: The LORD is the Maker of them all." Proverbs 22:2 (NIV)

"For the LORD gives wisdom, and from his mouth come knowledge and understanding." Proverbs 2:6 (NIV)

"By wisdom the LORD laid the earth's foundations, by understanding he set the heavens in place; by his knowledge the deeps were divided, and the clouds let drop the dew." Proverbs 3:19, 20 (NIV)

To the Child. God made everything. He planned the sky, the trees, and yes, you and me. God considered how to make everything perfect and pleasing to His sight. When He finished He said, "It is good!" I'm glad God did all of this so we would have such a nice place to live.

Additional Discussion

The encouragement found in the Scriptures should light our path in talking about God. Proverbs is filled with wisdom and knowledge. God is the Creator ... our Creator. To deny the fact that God created all things is to deny the very deity of God.

As Christian parents, we must lay a foundation which acknowledges God as Creator of the universe. Even today, there are those who deny this truth. They laugh at the existence of God. It is our responsibility to teach children God's truth from the Scriptures.

Summary

Throughout this entire chapter we have seen God stand forth as Creator, Father, Protector, Lord, our Alpha and Omega. God is our beginning and our end. He is the One who makes all life possible. God is the ultimate authority.

Always remember that the foundation laid wisely for God's work will be built upon by knowledge and understanding. We will not be baffled or amazed at our knowledge and understanding of God when we talk about Him. God supplies us with answers as we determine to acknowledge Him personally and openly. Sadly, God is nothing to those who refuse Him. They are wondering nomads in a spiritual vacuum. But to those of us who seek to know and understand Him, He is our Lord. He guides us along. He teaches us the things to say about Himself. He seasons our words and thoughts with insights which will allow our children to want to know more about God. He will point the way when we seek Him out.

Clearly, our task is to seek to learn more about God through reading the Scriptures and through prayer. God has something to share with each of us. Let us make a commitment to grow in knowledge of the Lord. We should be ready and willing to share Him with our children. Step forward in the confidence and security that God is ready to open the door of understanding to us as never before.

Mankind's first contact with God

Perhaps your youngster has asked, "Why do we need God? Why can't we do whatever we want without Him?" It is difficult for many boys and girls to understand just who God really is and why He is so interested in us. The reason for the confusion is easily understood since few children are told very much about God in their early years.

The answer is that we cannot live a full life, a meaningful life without Him. We were made for a special purpose. The mystery of our purpose is unraveled as we study the remainder of this chapter.

To the Adult. God created us for loving fellowship and to serve Him. We have been given special gifts by God. We are given brains capable of reasoning and making decisions which will affect our spiritual growth. We should use these resources to worship the God of love and reason—that's God's plan. When we are aware of God's plan for our lives it should be our goal to press that plan into action. As we allow our faith to function we mature as believers in Christ.

"Then God said, 'Let Us make man in Our image, according to Our likeness; and let them rule over the fish of the sea and over the birds of the sky and over the cattle and over all the earth, and over every creeping thing that creeps on the earth.' And God created man in His own image, in the image of God He created him; male and female He created them." Genesis 1:26, 27 (NAS)

God created us to love and communicate with Him. He made us with unique abilities to serve Him. We have dominion over fish, birds, cattle, and creeping things, over all the earth. We are servants of the living God. Consider the important place that God gave mankind; we are made in the image of God. We are to be like Him, seeking perfection and goodness.

God made us with minds, hearts and souls. We are special in the eyes of God. Let's ponder some Scriptures which give us additional insight concerning our relationship to God. It is wise to tuck these bits of knowledge into our hearts so we can share them at a chosen moment with our children.

David speaks in this psalm of God's creation of him, *"Your hands have made me and fashioned me; Give me understanding that I may learn Your commandments."* Psalms 119:73 (NKJV)

David knew without any doubt who created him. In his efforts to better himself, David asked God for understanding. We need God to provide us with understanding and knowledge of His ways and will for our lives. We are more than a creation of His, we are His adopted children through Jesus Christ our Lord.

Paul sets the record straight by clearly stating our relationship to the Father and to Jesus Christ, the Son of God. I think it is time for Christian people to understand there is more to salvation (eternal life) than being, "born again." We receive new life. *"You are all sons of God through faith in Christ Jesus, for all of you who were baptized into Christ have clothed yourselves with Christ. There is neither Jew nor Greek, slave nor free, male nor female, for you are all one in Christ Jesus. If you belong to Christ, then you are Abraham's seed, and heirs according to the promise."* Galatians 3:26-29 (NIV)

"How great is the love the Father has lavished on us, that we should be called children of God! And that is what we are!" 1 John 3:1 (NIV)

This verse clearly demonstrates how great God's love is for each of us through Jesus Christ our Lord and Savior. God cares!

It is vital to understand that God did not create us and leave us alone to "do our own thing." God has a plan for each life. If God has lavished His love upon us, so greatly, through Christ then surely there is a special challenge and opportunity to meet. It is only as we seek to understand God that we begin to unravel the mysteries of life and apply them wisely.

To the Child. God gave us a special blessing. Of all the things made by God, we are the only creatures that talk. God loves us so much that He still wants to know us and talk to us. Let's look at why God made us as found in Genesis 1:26,27. (Child's name), isn't it wonderful to belong to God? (Read and discuss Genesis 1:26,27 with your child.)

What does God teach us?

To the Adult. God has provided for all of mankind a set of strict values and standards. As your children begin to grow and experience life, certain truths will become reality:

- There is a right and wrong to everything.
- Not all people do what is fair and right.
- Some people take advantage of others whenever possible.
- There are good people and there are bad people.
- Not everyone is loving and kind.
- Some people will be unfair and unkind for almost any reason.
- Not all people go to Sunday School and church.
- Many people talk ugly and speak ungodly thoughts.
- There are many Christians who love Jesus and will love them too.
- Pushing and shoving is a way of life for many people.

You learn something new and valuable each day. Sometimes we learn the hard way, by experience. At nursery school, kindergarten, or grade school there are others who will oppose and reject your child. Perhaps your child has had only a limited amount of exposure to other children. Maybe the loving relationship within the family is all your youngster has experienced in the first few years. Whatever your child is like and no matter how protective you have been, remember he or she will meet the world head on very early in life. There's a lot to learn.

No matter how we strive to protect our children, they must learn how to live in a world that does not live by God's standards. This is a prime reason that we, as parents and friends, must introduce them to God. The worldly system distorts life and God's value system. The older the world grows, the more corrupt it seems to become. Not a pleasing thought but a truth that we must face. We can't wait! The time is now to teach our children about God's values. Tomorrow could be too late!

What, then, are some of the lessons that God desires us to learn?

1. Have faith and believe in God.
2. Accept God as part of your daily life.
3. Commit your ways to Him.
4. Obey God's standards.
5. Follow God.
6. Know and put into practice Christian principles.

At this point let's look at some of the basic beliefs your children should learn about God. Later on we will discuss how to help your child understand and accept Christ's gift of eternal life with Him. The first step is to learn to have faith and believe in God. To do this we must reflect upon some passages that teach about faith and believing. This is such an important topic, we will discuss it here and again in chapter ten.

Accept God as a part of your daily life

To the Adult. God is not some far-removed god like the gods worshipped by many other groups and societies. Our God is personal. He is alive. We need not build statues or temples to glorify Him. We need only believe in Him and allow Him to live within us.

As Christians, we know that God is with us at all times. He willingly lives within us through the Holy Spirit. We must recognize and treasure that fact. The Holy Spirit is ready to function as our spiritual guide. What comfort and joy we realize in the truth of this message, "the Holy Spirit lives within the soul of each Christian."

To the Child. Have you considered the joy it must give a willing heart as you tell your child, "child's name, God is always with us. Because He loves us and we love Him we know He is always near. Even though (child's name), you don't see Him, God is here. God wants you to know He loves you."

Additional Discussion

Always seek to display God as personal and real. Allow your child the privilege of expanding his or her faith and letting it function freely.

Never allow fear to overshadow your feelings about God. Children are eager to learn about God through your efforts. Remember they learn from you first. Your children have a need in their heart to love God as you do. Remember, always remain basic and simple when you talk about God being part of your life. We tend to make lessons about God more complex than necessary. Children don't need to be burdened with complex issues and doctrine in their search for Christ. *Be simple and basic!*

Commit your ways to God

To the Adult. How can children commit their ways to God? The answer isn't difficult. Young people should understand that to commit their ways and actions to God means they will allow God to show them right from wrong. That sounds as though it is greatly simplified, but it really isn't.

27

How do we know right from wrong? How are we sure that something is good or bad? Think about these questions for a moment. Get a piece of paper and a pencil and make a list of things which you know to be right. When you have completed this list, make a list of things you know to be wrong. How do you know the difference? God is at work in your life. He teaches you.

I recall a time when our daughter was struggling with some schoolmates. She wanted to be a part of a certain group, but she knew that if she wanted to become a member of "the club" she would have to do things she had been taught not to do. She decided not to join. God teaches us as we commit our ways to Him.

Likewise, our son faced a situation in which he felt there was no choice other than to "follow the crowd." In his heart he knew what to do, but the peer pressure was very strong. The children learned that each of us is taught by God, individually, the just and unjust things of life. God gives us freedom to make our own choices but God wants us to do what is right—the Bible makes that clear.

To the Child. Everything we do or say should show others that we love God. God knows what is best for us and He will show us right from wrong.

Obey God's standards

To the Adult. In this crazy, confused world, God's standards seem to have been pushed aside. Perhaps we should review a few of God's standards as found in the Scriptures. Standards are commandments and we need to teach them to our children.

The Ten Commandments
Taken from Exodus 20 (NIV)

1. *"You shall have no other gods before Me."* This Scripture tells us how God feels about putting something or someone else ahead of Him. He plainly says, "Don't do it! I am to be number one in your adoration and worship."

2. *"You shall not make for yourself an idol in the form of anything in heaven above or on the earth beneath or in the waters below."* You might find yourself wondering how to describe to your children what an idol is in today's world. Idols are: statues of other so-called gods; certain places of worship which are worshipped because they are sacred; possessions we have which are of supreme importance to us; and, anything which moves our concentration, beliefs and worship habits away from God.

3. *"You shall not misuse the name of the Lord your God, for the Lord will not hold anyone guiltless who misuses His name."* This commandment is especially painful for many people. How often do you hear the name of the Lord taken in vain? Frequently people curse the name of God as a matter of loose speech, a release of anger, or an expression of extreme displeasure.

Our children must realize that people who use the name of the Lord in vain are wrong. We need to aid them in bridging the gap and help them overcome the temptation to degrade the Lord's name as they often hear others do. We and our children need to learn to guard our tongues.

4. *"Remember the Sabbath day by keeping it holy."* This commandment has caused great conflict throughout the ages. How are we to judge what is right or wrong to do on the Holy Day? Who is to decide what can and cannot be done? How do we determine within our own family what we should or should not do? The matter is a personal one and I am in no position to judge. Read Exodus 20:8-11 and decide for yourself the standards by which you should conduct the Sabbath within your family. We do need to be sure that our children understand that the Sabbath is not just another day. It is a Holy Day set aside for rest and for worship of the Lord God. We seem endangered by the fast pace at which we live. It seems to snatch away our free moments and steal away those precious moments of quiet and privacy. We must budget our time and activities wisely. By no means should we ever

forget that God created the Sabbath as a time of rest, worship and consideration of Him. God expects it and we need it!

5. *"Honor your father and your mother, so that you may live long in the land the Lord your God is giving you."* It is extremely important that we remember to honor our parents and to love them. God has told us that we must do this—in fact, we should desire to live with this attitude. The person who cannot honor his or her parents seemingly has little room for love or anything else. Our parents were chosen by God. They guide us through those times of adjustment which begin on our first days. These are our God-given supporters until the day comes when we can stand on our own and make our own decisions.

In most lives, parents have made sacrifices and toiled very hard to provide for their children. Since I was raised during the 1940s and 1950s by parents who loved God, I learned a great deal about life. Times were hard for everyone! We were judged as almost poor by worldly standards. We seemed to have barely enough to get by. But my mother has said, "There were some hard times during and after World War II. I often wondered what we would do for the things we really needed. Somehow God provided the things we really needed to get by." My parents struggled and sacrificed for their children and I'll bet that most of your parents have done the same for you. I expect that most of you have struggled and sacrificed to some degree. It is a natural part of life. Our duty as parents is to provide the best opportunities we can for our children to get a good start in life. How do you honor your parents? Do you demonstrate the proper respect and loving attitude? Do you treat them in the manner in which you wish to be honored by your children? We owe our parents a special gift of love and respect. We should love our parents as God intended us to. In this way God will give us honor through our children.

6. *"You shall not murder."* This is a very controversial subject. Murder brings destruction and an untimely end to life. Consider what your children should know about murder and its effect. Think and pray about how to approach this sensitive subject. Help your youngster to appreciate life and hate murder.

Always recall that you are discussing God's view of murder, not your own. Tell your child why you think God has said not to murder. Why is murder wrong? What does murder do when it touches the lives of many? Be personal with your children. Be open and honest and express your feelings and concerns. Be sure you teach that murder is sinful in the eyes of God.

7. *"You shall not commit adultery."* For some of us this subject may be very difficult to approach. God has said, "Don't do it!" and yet adultery seems to run rampant, almost unchecked by our society. Adultery is sin! God said so. God has said that adultery is wrong no matter what circumstances it occurs under. Our "do-it-if-it-feels-good" society has swept the Ten Commandments under the carpet in order that people might do whatever their hearts desire. Consider God's value system when discussing this matter. Point out the dangers of compromising God's standards to fit today's life style.

8. *"You shall not steal."* What significant information have you given your child about stealing? The statistics concerning embezzlement, plagiarism, petty and grand larceny, stealing, and shoplifting are alarming. Throughout the world we appear to have an epidemic, of sorts, of taking things that don't belong to us. Dealing with this terrible problem has become a common occurrence for parents who once considered their children to be immune from stealing. Consider how many adults openly pilfer from the office or rob goods and services from one another. We have come to believe that this is not stealing at all but "taking what really belongs to us." God still labels it as stealing. Stealing is a sin and is wrong. As with the other commandments it is to be observed, not forgotten.

9. *"You shall not give false testimony against your neighbor."* The further we go in God's commandments the more difficult they seem to become and discuss. Right? Who gives false testimony? How do lies hurt others? Does your child understand how lies can destroy and tear apart lives? Have you considered how harmful a lie can be? Could lives be altered or changed

because someone bore false testimoney against someone else? Of course they could. It is important that we speak the truth.

We must begin to teach our children the value of truthfulness. Satan uses lies as tools to tear down lives and distort values. Lies only tear down, they never build up. Lies turn us toward the negative and cover up the positive influence in our lives. We should be certain our children learn to live life in the positive light of Christ and not in the shadow of negativity.

10. *"You shall not covet your neighbor's house."* I can almost hear you say, "Okay, what has that to do with me? This isn't a real problem area in my life; maybe with someone else, but not me!" Maybe you don't struggle with something of this nature. If you don't, consider yourself fortunate. But then again, I expect you have been caught in a trap similar to the one that seeks to ensnare me. At times, usually when I am tired or depressed, I am bothered by seeing people who have such nice homes. I see someone with a beautiful home with horses, cows and lots of green pastures. Something inside me wants it. I know we can't afford it but yet I covet it. Sometimes we become ensnared by objects such as fur coats, jewelry, cars, boats, or a multitude of other things. It might even be that we covet our neighbor's husband or wife.

There are many ways we struggle with coveting something someone else has. My example may be humorous to one person but to another it might be very realistic. If it was not for the fact that I strive to give all that concern over to the Lord, then my coverting would be my downfall. No doubt coveting can quickly lead us to sinful attitudes. We must be careful not to covet things. We usually don't need the things we covet anyway. Coveting is a worldly desire, not a spiritual need.

To the Child. You might say, "Mary Ann, you know rules are supposed to keep us from getting hurt. Well, God has given us rules to live by called the Ten Commandments. I want to show them to you." (Turn to the Scriptures and use the above discussion as a guide if you need it. Show your child what is right and what is wrong in God's terms.)

Then remind your child that when Jesus was asked which was the most important commandment, he answered, "The foremost is, 'Hear, O Israel! The Lord Our God Is One Lord; And you shall love the Lord your God with all your heart, and with all your soul, and with all your mind, and with all your strength.' The second is this, 'You Shall Love Your Neighbor As Yourself.' There is no other commandment greater than these." Mark 12:29-31 (NAS)

Additional Discussion

God has not left us to flounder in the mainstream of life without some guidelines and a lifeboat for safety. God is our Supreme Teacher. He hasn't forgotten us or left us to wander or stray into needless sin. Our problems are solved by centering our situation on God, not on worldly standards. The answers to life's greatest problems are solved through God. As believers in Christ we should hold fast to our faith. We need to grow in knowledge of the Scriptures and seek to learn more of God.

The fact is, the nearer we draw to God, the closer our relationship with Him becomes. Centering our lives around Him will close the door on many temptations. In discussing the Lord with our children we will find it easier to discuss actual events from our lives. If you find it too difficult to talk about God then you might reconsider your personal relationship with Him. The more personal your knowledge of God, the more freedom you will have with Him. Desire and expect to learn something fresh and exciting as you read and study your Bible on a daily basis. Let the Holy Spirit teach you through God's Word.

The Lord is our Master Teacher. He wants to show us how to live the abundant Christian life and share it freely with others. Let's get excited about sharing Christ with some of the most important people we know: our youth.

chapter three

The Trinity

Is there any more difficult question for us to address than "What is the Trinity?" As I have considered how to discuss this question a variety of other thoughts have entered my mind. Frankly, the Trinity is a very difficult subject to approach. You may want to postpone talking to your child about it until he or she becomes more mature and you feel more at ease discussing it. It is my hope this chapter will be both helpful and meaningful to you.

What Is the Trinity?

To the Adult. This is a question well worth pondering on a snowy night when you have nowhere to go and a great deal of time to think. It takes consideration and time to form opinions and conclusions as we speak of the Trinity. God has a tri-personal existence which is commonly referred to as the Trinity. The three parts of the Trinity are:

- God the Father
- God the Son
- God the Holy Spirit

To the Child. The Trinity is God the Father, God the Son, who we know as Jesus, and God the Holy Spirit, who is our friend and special helper.

God the Father:
Part One of the Trinity

To the Adult. God the Father is described in the Scriptures with this special emphasis. Turn to John 1:18 (NIV), *"No one has ever seen God, but God the only Son, who is at the Father's side, has made Him known."*

"In the beginning God created the heavens and the earth." Genesis 1:1 (NAS) This passage states the truth that from the beginning God has been whom He says he is: God.

"Yet for us there is one God, the Father, from whom all things came and for whom we live; and there is but one Lord, Jesus Christ, through whom all things came and through whom we live." 1 Corinthians 8:6 (NIV)

Jesus gave us some additional insight into the subject at hand. *"Jesus answered and said to him, 'If anyone loves Me, he will keep My word; and My Father will love him, and We will come to him and make Our home with him. He who does not love Me does not keep My words; and the word which you hear is not Mine but the Father's who sent Me. These things I have spoken to you while being present with you. But the Helper, the Holy Spirit, whom the Father will send in My name, He will teach you all things, and bring to your remembrance all things that I said to you.'"* John 14:23-26 (NKJV)

To the Child. Remember, (child's name), God is the beginning of all life. He made all of us. (Discuss the Scriptures given above with your child.)

Additional Discussion

This subject of the Trinity can foster tremendous theological discussion. But since ours is not a theological study we won't dive into these deep waters. Instead we will only wade in up to our ankles. As you consider the Trinity it is important to let your faith function and not allow the unexplainable mysteries of God to overwhelm you. We, as human beings, are not capable of reasoning through these mysteries. In fact, this is not the purpose of our study at all. Ours is to teach our youngsters the value of believing and trusting in God. They learn to believe the Bible by our assurance and trust that God's Word is factual and has been proven throughout the centuries.

God the Son:
Part Two of the Trinity

To the Adult. Jesus is the Son of God. There are many who would discredit this claim. But God has confirmed this clearly throughout the Bible. To deny that Jesus Christ is the Son of God is to say that God has misrepresented His Son to us.

"And the Word became flesh, and dwelt among us, and we beheld His glory, glory as of the only begotten from the Father, full of grace and truth." John 1:14 (NAS)

"But of the Son He says, 'THY THRONE, O GOD, IS FOR-EVER AND EVER, AND THE RIGHTEOUS SCEPTER IS THE SCEPTER OF HIS KINGDOM.'" Hebrews 1:8 (NAS)

"And those who were in the boat worshipped Him, saying, 'You are certainly God's Son!'" Matthew 14:33 (NAS) As we know, only God is to be worshipped. Recall the commandments of God. Jesus would never have allowed such a remark to go unchallenged if it were not true. Christ works in truth and in fact.

It is certain that Christ forgave and still forgives sins. We know that only God can forgive sin, for the Bible reaffirms this truth time and time again. Read Mark 2:5-11 for reference. And we know that Jesus claimed authority in heaven and on earth. (Matthew 28:18) We are also taught that Jesus walked upon the waters of Galilee. The wind and waves of the sea obeyed His command to be still. Jesus had authority over the elements. No human can completely control the elements. Jesus is a vital part of the Trinity, the Son.

To the Child. Jesus is the Son of God. He is also one with God. Jesus has always existed. Jesus and the Father are one yet we also think of Them as Father and Son. Jesus, for the time He was on earth, gave up His home in heaven with the Father. Jesus came to earth and became a man, but yet He was also still God. Think of that! God, Jesus, loved us enough to come down and be like one of the creatures that He created. Jesus, Son of God and Son of Man, came to earth so that we could see the Father and know what the Father was like. Jesus said, "He who has seen me has seen the Father."

The Holy Spirit:
The Third Part of the Trinity

To the Adult. We have had a brief glimpse of Jesus' words concerning the coming of the Helper. The Helper is, of course, the Holy Spirit. One of the best-kept secrets of the Christian life appears to be the Holy Spirit. You may have heard the term "The Holy Ghost." As a child this term tended to frighten me. Parents, it will be of great benefit to your children if they can understand the terms used in describing the Holy Spirit, as well as the function of the Holy Spirit.

"I will give you a new heart and put a new spirit in you; I will remove from you your heart of stone and give you a heart of flesh. And I will put My Spirit in you and move you to follow my decrees and be careful to keep My laws." Ezekiel 36:26,27 (NIV)

"If you love me, you will obey what I command. And I will ask the Father, and he will give you another Counselor to be with you forever—the Spirit of Truth. The world cannot accept him, because it neither sees him nor knows him. But you know him, for he lives with you and will be in you." John 14:15—18 (NIV)

"Don't you know that you yourselves are God's temple and that God's Spirit lives in you? If anyone destroys God's temple, God will destroy him; for God's temple is sacred, and you are that temple." 1 Corinthians 3:16,17 (NIV)

Pretty strong words, aren't they? As you talk with your children, these beautiful words should be encouraging as well as enlightening. What a beautiful truth to learn at a young age. The Spirit of God lives within the Christian. In discussing this idea build on it a little, day by day. When your Christian children know and understand that a part of God lives in them, they should be glad and happy. Through your efforts to help them understand, they can feel secure in their faith.

Function of the Holy Spirit

What, then, is the main function of the Holy Spirit? Jesus stated the message clearly in the verses above. Here is yet another verse concerning the Holy Spirit which should be shared with your children.

"And I will pray to the Father, and He will give you another Helper, that He may abide with you forever, even the Spirit of

truth, whom the world cannot receive because it neither sees Him nor knows Him; but you know Him, for He dwells with you and will be in you." John 14:16,17 (NKJV)

To the Child. The Holy Spirit is God's special gift to Christians. The Holy Spirit is God's Spirit living deep inside you and me. We can't see Him because He is a spirit, but we can know He is there and is ready to help us. We know this because the Bible teaches us about Him and as we grow closer to God we will sense His Spirit in us.

Additional Discussion

The passage above (John 14:16,17) speaks of the word (those who do not know because they will not believe in or receive Christ as Savior). You might want to talk with your child regarding the contrast between those who believe and those who do not. This is the perfect moment to set this fact in your child's mind.

We know, but our children have yet to learn, that those who do not believe in Christ feel that our faith is senseless. There are those who scoff and ridicule our faith. The explanation for their reaction is that they have been spiritually blinded by Satan. Build your children's confidence and Christian character with words which enable them to understand that their faith in Christ is correct. Share the circumstances surrounding your own personal walk with Christ. Permit them to ask questions. Confide in them with the attitude that God will shed light on your conversation. Use your personal walk to help your children learn to know Christ personally and to accept Him as the Lord and Savior of their lives too. He will honor your efforts as you share your faith.

Secondly, this passage relates information concerning the Holy Spirit (called the Helper in this passage) and where the Spirit is found. There can be no doubt that Christians have a unique Helper. He is sent with a special purpose. Children should be taught that the Helper is a special friend (a term they can easily understand) sent by our loving God. This interpretation of the Scripture demonstrates the depths of God's love. Not only did God send His precious Son, Jesus Christ, to help us, but He also provided the Holy Spirit. That's good news for all people.

How to Explain the Trinity

To the Adult and Child. As simply as possible, please! Here are two examples you might consider using. When you cut an apple in three parts, each part looks somewhat different. One section might contain mostly seeds, another section the stem, and the third the core. If you put the pieces back together, as they were cut, they still make an apple. So it is with the Trinity; all the parts are separate, but each has a purpose and a function. When you put the pieces of the Trinity together, you have a perfect picture of the character of God.

The second example is to use yourself. I will use myself as an example in this illustration. I am a wife, a mother and a daughter. To my parents, I am their third child. I am also their youngest child. I am very different than my older brother and my older sister. However, if my parents were to speak of me, they might say, "Our daughter Frances."

I am my husband's wife. I am the girl who married Sandy Carroll over twenty years ago. When we married I took his name and became his wife. He sees me as his lifelong partner. There we have the second part of Frances Loftiss Carroll, Sandy's wife.

Third, I am very definitely a mother. Ray and Mary Ann are the two children I gave birth to. Sometimes as a mother there are other things I do for them but I am still their mom. Nothing will change that; I am forever the mother of those two children.

All these persons form a part of me. While my life is composed of a variety of functions and each person views me a bit differently, I am still Frances Carroll. My personality is a blend of daughter, wife, and mother. So it is with God. Each part of the Trinity is completely unique and separate, but yet in its completeness it gives us a clear picture of God. Complete, whole and entirely God; that's the Trinity.

chapter four

Jesus Christ, the Son of God

Now that we have laid a foundation of faith, we will begin to explore the one who gave us new life: Jesus Christ. The world (those who do not believe in Jesus as the Christ) attempts to discredit our Lord. That's not unexpected, however, for the Scriptures acknowledge that fact. Ours, as believers in Christ, is to remain steadfast in our beliefs and to share those ideas with our youngsters.

A Promise from God

To the Adult. God made a special provision for mankind, and for our sinfulness: *"Therefore the Lord Himself will give you a sign: Behold, a virgin will be with child and bear a son, and she will call His name Immanuel."* Isaiah 7:14 (NAS). God sent His Son to redeem us from evildoing.

When Adam and Eve fell into sin in the Garden of Eden,

Satan won a slight victory. He was inventive enough to tempt and mislead man and woman into wrong doing. Satan knew that God would tolerate no sin in His presence, for God is perfect; thus, Adam and Eve would be punished. They were banished from the garden. Satan was not the final victor in this situation, however, for God had made a plan. (Satan can do nothing without God's permission. If it appears that Satan has temporarily triumphed, remember that God had to permit it. If God permits it, then it will fit into His overall plan and sovereign will.)

God sent His perfect Son, Jesus Christ, as a substitute for man's sinful past, present, and future. With Christ as our Redeemer, the only one who could free us from the yoke of sin, God would forgive our sins and provide perfect grace (atonement for our sins through Christ's blood sacrifice) through His Son, Jesus Christ our Lord and Savior.

Christ, God's promised purification for our sins, restores our relationship with God the Father. Christ is our mediator, our substitute for death because of sin. Christ gives new life.

To the Child. When Adam and Eve disobeyed God in the Garden of Eden, sin entered the world. God can't have sin in His presence. Therefore, because of Adam's and Eve's sin (disobedience), man could not enjoy being close to God like he was before sin. There was nothing that man could do himself to make up for the wrong he had done. So God promised to send His own Son, Jesus, to take the punishment that man deserved so we could be close to God again.

The Virgin Birth

To the Adult. The current trend seems to make it fashionable to deny the virgin birth. To contradict the Scriptures is to call God a liar. God is no liar! In a world that is set against God there are many who blatantly declare that Christ was not born of a virgin. To say such a thing is blasphemy. God will not allow those who attempt to blemish His Son's life to go without harsh punishment. Because the bulk of humanity lives by a false set of standards, people seek to bend and twist Christ to fit their plan. They seek to make Christ less than perfect. Satan is still at work attempting to discredit Christ.

It will never work! Christ is the author and perfecter of our faith. He is God's grace, which flows freely to all who accept the gift of salvation offered by Christ. We will consider this fact in depth a little further on in this study. Stand firm in relating the message of Christ accurately so that your child will know that the complete story of Christ, as presented in the Bible, is accurate and totally reliable.

"Now in the sixth month the angel Gabriel was sent from God to a city in Galilee, called Nazareth, to a virgin, engaged to a man whose name was Joseph, of the descendants of David; and the virgin's name was Mary. And coming in, he said to her, 'Hail, favored one! The Lord is with you.' But she was greatly troubled by this statement and kept pondering what kind of salutation this might be. And the angel said to her, 'Do not be afraid, Mary; for you have found favor with God, and behold you will conceive in your womb, and bear a son, and you shall name Him Jesus. He will be great, and will be called the Son of the Most High; and the Lord God will give Him the throne of His father David; and He will reign over the house of Jacob forever; and His kingdom will have no end.' And Mary said to the angel, 'How can this be, since I am a virgin?' And the angel answered and said to her, 'The Holy Spirit will come upon you, and the power of the Most High will overshadow you; and for that reason the holy offspring shall be called the Son of God.'" (Luke 1:26-35 NAS)

To comment on this section of Scripture would prove fruitless on my part. God has set the record straight. He has told it "like it is" so that we will not be confused by outside influences.

"Now all this took place that what was spoken by the Lord through the prophet might be fulfilled, saying, 'BEHOLD, THE VIRGIN SHALL BE WITH CHILD, AND SHALL BEAR A SON, AND THEY SHALL CALL HIS NAME IMMANUEL,' which translated means, 'GOD WITH US.' And Joseph arose from his

45

sleep, and did as the angel of the Lord commanded him, and took her as his wife, and kept her a virgin until she gave birth to a Son; and he called His name Jesus." Matthew 1:22-25 (NAS)

There can be *no compromises* in this teaching. As you discuss God's plan with your children, make sure you state this idea clearly. God's plans cannot be altered and degraded to fit mankind's standards:

Let's examine these verses to see just how complete the plan was:

- God sent an angel to Nazareth to carry the message of His plan.
- The angel made clear God's arrangements for Mary.
- Joseph understood and accepted the instructions of the angel.

He did not doubt or turn aside from the instructions given him. He knew that God had made him responsible for Mary's future.

- Mary and Joseph accepted God's arrangement and obeyed God.

You may be certain that while they did not fully comprehend all the details of God's plan they did what God had instructed them to do. Consider the questions they must have had and the mystery of it all. Mary was chosen to be the mother of God's son, Jesus Christ. What joy she must have felt in her heart and yet there were many things she did not understand.

- Both Joseph and Mary allowed their faith in God to come forth.

It would have been easy to waver or run away but they did not. They were sensitive to God's call to share their lives with Him to the fullest. They accepted the greatest challenge of all, that of raising the Son of God.

To the Child. God, and only God, was the Father of Jesus. Mary was a young girl who had not yet married. God worked a miracle in Mary's life and she gave birth to God's only Son, Jesus Christ.

Events of The Birth and
The Childhood of Jesus Christ

To the Adult. Why is it that we seem to tell the story of Jesus' birth only at Christmas? We seem to store it for a special season. Shouldn't it be told more often? What joy we experience as we share the "Christmas story" with our children. When children think of Jesus' birth it should bring happiness to their hearts. Maybe the glimmering tinsel and the beautifully decorated tree in the living room aren't all that important after all. Maybe the twinkle in your children's eyes is there because of their belief in Christ.

Perhaps you can work the "Chistmas story" into a conversation while you take a walk with your children. Even when you are giving your youngster a bath you can take the time to share a very special story. The opportunities are limitless. The times when you are natural and are being yourself are when you set the best examples for your children.

Consider the story as found in Luke 2:1-20. Allow me to share it with you in the following manner:

Jesus Is Born

Just before Jesus was born there was an order sent down from the ruler, Caesar Augustus, to take a count of all of the people in the region and their properties. To do this each person had to go to the city of his or her origin.

Joseph, a carpenter from Nazareth, had his family ties in Bethlehem. Joseph was from the house, or family, of David. So Joseph had to travel from his home in Nazareth to Bethlehem to register. He took Mary, his promised wife, with him. Mary, as we know, was about to give birth to a special child, God's child, Jesus Christ.

When the couple arrived in the area the city was very, very crowded. Many people had come from faraway places to register their names and belongings, just as Mary and Joseph had. The streets were filled with people. There was no place for Mary and Joseph to stay. Joseph looked everywhere. He knew Mary needed rest. She looked so weary and it had been a difficult trip for her. Joseph was very concerned about his wife.

Joseph's spirits sagged when his efforts to locate a place to rest failed. Even when there was no room for them at the smallest inn, Joseph knew that there had to be a place where Mary could rest. As Joseph spoke to the innkeeper his words must have filled the man's heart with compassion and kindness. The innkeeper made a place for them in the stable.

When the time came for Mary to give birth to her son, she wrapped Him in cloth and laid Him in a manger. Mary was very proud of the beautiful little baby. She loved her new son and was glad that God had chosen her to be His mother. Imagine what Mary must have thought about God's choosing her to be Jesus' mother. What an honor! God had chosen her, an ordinary young woman, to be Jesus' mother. What joy must have filled her heart as she hugged her baby.

THE SHEPHERDS

As you and I know, there were shepherds in the fields, watching over their sheep. It was a thankless job, but it had to be done. It was a clear night and the stars danced and twinkled with a special message.

An angel of the Lord appeared to the shepherds from out of nowhere. The shepherds trembled, not from the chill of the evening but from fear. Think about how frightened you and I would be if an angel of the Lord appeared to us. I think our knees would knock together like cymbals in a marching band. We would tremble because we wouldn't understand why the angel had come. But this angel had a special message that soon put the shepherds at ease.

The angel's first words were words of comfort to the shepherds. "Don't be afraid. I bring you some very good news." Imagine how eager the shepherds were to hear what the angel had to say. "Today in the city of David, Bethlehem, a Savior has been born who is Christ the Lord." This was happy news for the shepherds for they had long awaited the arrival of their Savior. God had promised He would come, and now He was here.

The shepherds wondered how they would know the child. After all, there were many babies in the area. "This will be a sign for you," the angel said. "When you locate the baby He will be wrapped in swaddling clothes and sleeping in a manger." Then a multitude of heavenly hosts appeared, all of them praising God and saying, "Glory to God in the highest, and on earth peace, good will toward all men!"

Suddenly there was silence. The angel and the heavenly hosts disappeared. Their news excited the shepherds, who left in haste to find the Savior as they reflected upon the words they had heard.

It was as the angel had said when they found Mary, Joseph, and the baby. The baby lay in the manger, with His mother nearby. As the shepherds spoke, telling Mary and Joseph what had happened to them, Mary stored the words away in her heart. Their words filled her with even greater happiness as she remembered them throughout the years.

THE VISIT OF THE WISE MEN

We often confuse children when we tell the story of Jesus' birth. We tend to give the impression that Mary and Joseph arrived in Bethlehem and that all of the events took place within a matter of a few hours. Frankly, I think we should make sure our children understand that all of these events took some time. Who knows how long? Not I. But you can be sure it took time for the wise men to journey to Bethlehem from their faraway homeland. Don't cram all of the facts together; allow your children to experience the joy of Jesus' birth and the angel's announcement to the fullest. Don't rush Jesus' birth so that you can hurry on to something else. It's far too important a matter and it is difficult for a child's mind to sort out. Careless actions on the part of a parent, grandparent, or teacher might confuse a child for a lifetime. Help your children gain a proper perspective by helping them to understand that God had to work in many places at the same time to cause this beautiful story to come together.

When the Magi arrived from the east and entered the city of Jerusalem, King Herod wondered why they had come. He had no knowledge of the birth of the King of the Jews. When he heard the news he set his plan into action. Herod intended to have the Magi bring news of this King of the Jews and then he would have the child murdered. Herod was a jealous king. He desired to be the sole ruler of the people.

The Magi must have realized that they had made a serious mistake when they confided in Herod. He knew nothing of the babe or the special star that twinkled in the sky. With the information gained from scribes and priests as to where Christ was to be born, the Magi departed for that region. Although they told Herod they would return with information about Christ, they never did. They understood the danger the child was in and wanted no part of Herod's evil plan.

When they came to the place where Mary and the child were they rejoiced. They fell down and worshipped Him. They knew without any doubt that this was the promised Savior. I expect their hearts were filled with joy and their eyes with tears as they worshipped Christ the Lord.

It was not enough to praise and worship the child. They had brought gifts to honor Him: gold, frankincense, and myrrh.

Mary and Joseph must have been overwhelmed by these gifts. These were gifts fit for a king, and this child was indeed a King. This child, God's Son, came to change the world and to alter the course of sin and wickedness. Jesus came to forgive us for our sins and to free us from the grasp of the evil things in our lives.

To the Child. The story of Jesus' birth is a beautiful story and it's all true. God cares so much for us that He sent His only Son to live here for a while. Let's read the story together. (Read the story of Jesus Christ's birth with your child.)

I realize that my story of Jesus' birth is lengthy and goes into a great deal of detail, but children need to know more about Jesus.

We need to evaluate the importance of Christ's birth. It is the cornerstone for building knowledge and a belief in Christ as Lord and Savior.

Allow your boy or girl to realize this: From the very beginning of Jesus' life and even before His birth, Jesus was unique. God chose to send Jesus to the earth so that we might know more about God's love for mankind. Jesus is more than most of us give Him credit for being. God changed the entire world through Jesus Christ. For those who will accept Christ, there is reason to be glad and to praise the name of the Lord.

Jesus Grows Up

To the Adult. We all know that the Bible reveals little about the childhood of Jesus. When our children ask us to tell them what Jesus was like as a baby or a young boy, what can we say?

Jesus was like any other little baby. He cried, laughed, and had tummy aches too.

Jesus learned to crawl, toddle and walk just like you did. He fell down and skinned His knees like all children do when they are small.

As a small boy, Jesus had times when He didn't feel good and got sick. I expect Jesus even had a virus from time to time. You see, while Jesus was special, He was also human like you and me. Because He was like you and me, Jesus knew what it was like to be hurt and to cry. Jesus even knew about being disliked by other people.

Jesus played with other children. He played games much like you play games with your friends. (Child name), what kind of games do you think He played? Do you think Jesus was a "good sport" or a "sore loser?"

Jesus had brothers and sisters too. He liked people and was fun to be with. Imagine (child's name), what it would have been like to share a room with Jesus. Do you think His room was anything like yours?

Jesus never allowed anything He did to cause Him to get into trouble. Jesus knew right from wrong. He was taught right from wrong and knew what to do and what not to do. God teaches us right from wrong too, (child's name).

Jesus studied His lessons. How well? Consider Jesus in the temple with the elders at age 12. He knew enough about His lessons to speak with knowledge to the elders.

Jesus helped at home. When Jesus was assigned chores, He did them. Furthermore, He didn't grumble and complain when His mother asked Him to do something. He was a willing helper.

Jesus learned a trade. He learned how to work with His hands. Jesus learned to be a carpenter as Joseph showed Him how to make things from various kinds of wood. Consider how handy this must have been during His adult years. Surely there were times, although they aren't recorded in the Scriptures, when Jesus used His abilities and talents to help meet the needs of those around Him.

Jesus grew strong. He grew to be a man just like any boy does. He experienced the same things all boys experience. He had growing pains and aches, and Jesus was a lot like any boy. The only difference was that Jesus was the Son of God.

To the Child. Jesus grew to be a man like all young boys do. He felt many of the same feelings all people do. He laughed, joked, cried, and experienced moments of struggle. Jesus' life was not without problems, but Jesus never did anything wrong.

HUMANNESS OF JESUS CHRIST

To the Adult. There are many who wish to overlook the fact that Jesus possessed the same characteristics and emotions that you and I do. They pretend not to notice that Jesus felt, acted, and responded in a human fashion. If He had not been both human and divine it would have been impossible for Jesus to offer His life in sacrifice for our sins.

Because Jesus knew what it meant to be human then He knew all about struggles and joys. Let's focus on some facts about Jesus as He lived here on earth.

We need not confuse our children any more than necessary

when we explain the fact that Jesus Christ was both natural and supernatural. What we must try to do in this area of study is to allow our children to see Jesus as a special man, God's Son. We can guide them to an understanding later that Jesus was God as a part of the Trinity, but for now let's think about Jesus as a flesh-and-blood man. Not just an ordinary man, but a man with the power of God at His disposal.

"And I will put enmity between you and the woman, and between your offspring and hers; he will crush your head, and you will strike his heel." Genesis 3:15 (NIV)

This verse relays the conversation between God and the serpent. God foretells the future birth of Christ. Christ had, as we know, had an earthly mother, Mary. You see, God had planned for Christ to come and free us from Adam and Eve's fall.

To the Child. Jesus was just as real as you or I. He was both human and divine.

JESUS AS A SERVANT

To the Adult. *"Just as the Son of Man did not come to be served, but to serve, and to give his life as a ransom for many."* Matthew 20:28 (NIV)

Christ came to serve mankind. When we learn the things that Jesus did we clearly see the truth of this statement. No one person has done more for mankind than has our Lord. His concern has always been for others first, Himself last. Throughout the Gospels He teaches, heals, and shares freely the love of God. Jesus lived in accordance with God's standards, not by worldly standards. The things Jesus taught set mankind's system on its ear. Jesus lived life to the fullest, never asking, "What's in it for Me?" Rather His life was lived as a servant to all of mankind.

There is so much more to learn about Jesus. We must press on in our efforts to discuss Him with our children. Our study turns now to concentrate more on Jesus' unselfishness and willingness to serve. Jesus was God. He could have been the Master—

He didn't have to be a servant. In fact the Jews expected Christ to come as a ruling King, not as a servant.

Why is it important that we understand Matthew 20:28? What spiritual insight is there that we must grasp? Just what is it that a servant does?

- A servant puts the one who is served ahead of his or her own needs or desires.
- A servant is considerate.
- A servant is sensitive to the needs of others.
- A servant watches carefully.

Is there something left undone? Is there some little something which would make a difference if it were done?

- A good servant does special things without being asked.
- A good servant isn't content with doing an adequate job but with doing the best job at all times.
- A servant who is concerned for others receives joy when the job has been "well done."
- A servant wants the ones he or she serves to be comfortable.

These are but a few of the thoughts of what a good servant does. There are many more. Perhaps some others have come to mind. But the main point is that Christ considered Himself as a servant of mankind. His work was done as God's volunteer. He always sought to be our special helper. Christ was consistently striving to share with others so that others might come to know God through Him.

There is no doubt that Jesus stirred up the entire system of the day. He lived life in a different mode with a different perspective than was common to the lifestyle of that day or our time. Jesus was concerned about each individual person. He sought to make Himself available whenever possible. His goal was for us to know and comprehend that God had sent Him as the promised Messiah.

To the Child. Study the material given above for the adult. Think about examples that you can give comparing Jesus' humanity to that of your child. Explain to your child what a servant is and what it means to be a servant of God. Remember that Jesus was human and He was also God. Have you ever thought about the fact that when Jesus served the disciples by washing their feet that that was God stopping to wash the feet of men He created? Use that example when explaining how Jesus wants us to serve one another.

JESUS CHRIST AND COMPASSION

To the Adult. Where do we begin as we discuss compassion with our children? There is so much that Jesus did that demonstrated compassion.

Jesus wept more than once. This knowledge is ours as we read the Scriptures for ourselves and learn that Christ was truly a concerned person.

"As he approached Jerusalem and saw the city, he wept over it and said, 'If you, even you, had only known on this day what would bring you peace—but now it is hidden from your eyes. The day will come upon you when your enemies will build an embankment against you and encircle you and hem you in on every side. They will dash you to the ground, you and the children within your walls. They will not leave one stone on another, because you did not recognize the time of God's coming to you.'" Luke 19:41-44 (NIV)

What has Jesus in the passages we have just read? Clearly His words continue to ring throughout the ages: "You did not recognize the time of God's coming to you, Jerusalem." They turned aside and refused to believe that Jesus Christ was the One, the Chosen One, the Messiah that God had long promised.

How sad our Lord must have felt. His heart was moved and his spirit was weighed with concern for these people. How He wanted them to understand His message. Now the time was near that He would die for our sins upon the cross at Calvary. Jesus had a "heart burden," a deep burden for those who refused to accept Him as their Lord and Savior. He still has this same attitude; Christ cares and is concerned for all people.

"Then, when Mary came where Jesus was, and saw Him, she fell down at His feet, saying to Him, 'Lord, if You had been here, my brother would not have died.' Therefore, when Jesus saw her weeping, and the Jews who came with her weeping, He groaned in the spirit and was troubled. And He said, 'Where have you laid him?' They said to Him, 'Lord, come and see.' Jesus wept. Then the Jews said, 'See how He loved him.' And some of them said, 'Could not this Man, who opened the eyes of the blind, also have kept this man from dying?' Then Jesus, again groaning in Himself, came to the tomb. It was a cave, and a stone lay against it. Jesus said, 'Take away the stone.' Martha, the sister of him who was dead, said to Him, 'Lord, by this time there is a stench, for he has been dead four days.' Jesus said to her, 'Did I not say to you that if you would believe you would see the glory of God?' Then they took away the stone from the place where the dead man was lying. And Jesus lifted up His eyes and said, 'Father, I thank You that You have heard Me. And I know that You always hear Me, but because of the people who are standing by I said this, that they may believe that You sent Me.' Now when He had said these things, He cried with a loud voice, 'Lazaraus, come forth!' And he who had died came out bound hand and foot with grave clothes, and his face was wrapped with a cloth. Jesus said to them, 'Loose him, and let him go.'" John 11:32-44 (NKJV)

There are several reasons we should discuss this story with our children.

1. Parents, please heed this special warning. Don't focus on the idea that "Jesus wept" is the shortest verse in the Bible. That's true but that's only a small part of the story.

2. Jesus was concerned when He saw Mary approach. Mary had allowed her grief to overwhelm her trust in Christ. She knew the truth, as she saw it. Her brother was dead. Grief is a personal struggle with emotions and needs. Mary missed her brother. Death often brings the feelings of "if only." If only I could see him or her again. If only I could tell him or her that I love him or her. If only there was one more day. Grief cuts deeply to our innermost self. It hurts! It causes us to reflect back and we know there is nothing we can do to change the situation. No matter how strong our faith in the Lord, all are touched by the grief process sooner or later. It hurts to lose someone you love.

Jesus saw this attitude in Mary and in those who mourned with her. He was touched. He knew the struggle within His own heart as He considered the death of His friend, Lazarus. Jesus was aware of what He would and could do in this situation and yet Jesus still wept.

3. Jesus wept. Knowing that death is only a temporary adjustment for those of us who believe in Christ as Lord and Savior— Jesus still wept. Why? There are several reasons I feel that Jesus was moved to tears.

- Jesus felt the anguish sorrow brings.
- Jesus knew that separation from a loved one is painful.
- Jesus had compassion and felt sympathy for the family.
- Jesus knew the temporary loss of a special friend.
- Jesus experienced the grief that death brings.
- Jesus wept for reasons unexplained but felt deeply within.
- Jesus loved this man and felt the searching in His heart that all feel who have lost a loved one.

But Jesus was not without hope. Jesus was in full control of the situation and acted with confidence. Jesus spoke openly with His Father, God, in order that those present might reaffirm their trust and faith in Him. These people were to learn that death was but a temporary loss. While Lazarus was raised from the dead those present witnessed that death had no hold over the powers of God.

In discussing this story please reassure your children that for those who love the Lord Jesus Christ death brings a new beginning. It is my belief that we pass from this life into an immediate presence with Jesus Christ. I believe that in a split second from the time we take our last breath here, we take our first steps in our new life in eternity. Christ has promised that as we leave the presence of life here that He will be with us. For the believer there should be no greater message than this. After all, this is part of Christ's gift to us and we should be happy to know it is awaiting all of us.

To the Child. Jesus had a heart filled with love and compassion. He cared very deeply about each person. He wanted everyone to understand God. This means, Ray (child's name), we will want to always try to do what is right so we will honor God as His child. We need to have love and concern for those around us. We should learn to put other people's problems ahead of ours.

JESUS THE HEALER

Throughout the gospels there is evidence that Christ healed men, women, and children. Matthew 15:30,31 (NAS), "And great multitudes came to Him, bringing with them those who were lame, crippled, blind, dumb, and many others, and they laid down at His feet; and He healed them, so that the multitude marveled as they saw the dumb speaking, the crippled restored, and the lame walking, and the blind seeing; and they glorified the God of Israel."

To the Adult. Multitudes of people sought to be near Christ. He healed because He loved. He made them whole and complete again. There were some who needed physical healing while others needed spiritual help. One of these was the demonic, our next case study.

To the Child. Jesus called on God's powers at all times. As God's chosen helper, Jesus Christ healed many who were sick, blind, lame and deaf. Jesus performed these miracles so that the people would know God had sent Jesus as His messenger. Jesus did everything He could to demonstrate God's love and compassion to all of mankind.

JESUS' AUTHORITY OVER EVIL

To the Adult. *"When they reached the crowd, a man came up to Him, kneeling before Him and saying, 'Lord, do pity my son, for he has epilepsy and suffers excruciating pain, and often falls into the fire or into the water. I brought him to your disciples, and they could not cure him.' And Jesus answered, 'O you unbelieving and perverted people of the times! How long can I put up with you? Bring him here to me!' And Jesus reproved the demon, and it came out of him, and the boy was cured that very moment."* Matthew 17:14-18 (Williams)

Our mental and physical well-being is of importance to the Lord. Nothing is too complex or complicated for Christ. Notice in the pasages above that Jesus spoke sternly to the evil spirit. Evil spirits and demonic influence have no power when in full contention with Jesus Christ. Nothing is stronger than the power of God.

To the Child. Jesus spoke with the authority of God. When Jesus commanded evil to leave a person it must be done. There is no power greater than the power of God. As a Christian, you should know that there is nothing that can keep God from achieving the results He desires in our life. Satan must obey God when He speaks. You should realize that Satan tries to pull a lot of bluffs in our lives and we do not have to give in to wrong.

chapter five

Jesus' Gift

For the one who seeks to know Christ in depth, this chapter will be an exciting one. Talking about Jesus Christ, our Lord and Savior, can be a great deal of fun, especially as we pave the way of understanding for a child to come to know Him as Savior.

Children are curious about Jesus. Consider how often you have had questions concerning Jesus and had no one who could answer them. This chapter should be helpful to all who read it, for none of us can ever learn *too much* about Jesus.

Forgiveness

"Mom, will you forgive me? Dad, I've done wrong, will you ever forgive me?" Have you ever heard these questions? More than likely if you haven't, you will.

Please, parent, grandparent, or friend, a child can be sensitive to the Holy Spirit as you discuss forgiveness. When you tell your child that God forgives please allow the child to understand that this forgiveness is total and complete. Remember, no strings attached!

When your child says, "I am sorry" and asks for forgiveness he or she should understand that God completely forgives because of Jesus. Jesus offered His perfect life as a sacrifice for our sins and wrong doings. Without Christ there is no forgiveness of sin. But because Jesus is perfect and took our sins with Him to the cross, we can be forgiven. The child should be content with the idea that God does forgive the Christian because Jesus paid the penalty of our sin when He died. That is, after all, why Jesus came. Jesus came to free us from sin's grasp on us.

To the Child. I know that asking someone to forgive you when you have made a mistake isn't easy. But when you ask forgiveness you are free from that awful guilty feeling you have inside. God forgives us when we ask Him to and is very pleased that we want to set the record straight. God gives us another chance to begin again when we ask for forgiveness.

The Power of Sin: Then and Now

To the Adult. To understand the gift that Jesus Christ has given us, let's review some of the past and glance into the future. There are many interesting passages which talk about the power of sin in our lives. Below is a list of some passages you might want to look up. Since our space is limited we cannot print the entire text of each verse.

- David's prayer concerning his sinfulness: Psalms 51
- Sin is lawlessness: 1 John 3:4

- Facts about sin: 1 John 3:6-9
- What Jesus said concerning sin: John 8:34-36
- Willful sin: Hebrews 10:26,27
- The contrast between death in Adam and life in Christ: Romans 5-6

Over and over again the Scriptures reaffirm our human weakness. In talking about sin remember to reassure your child with the fact that in our weakness, Christ is our hope and strength.

Sin turns our attention from God to ourselves. The more inclined we are to sin the further we drift from God. God, as you and I know, cannot tolerate our sinful state. The more selfish our hearts become the less we seek out the loving Father until finally we become calloused and hardened. Sinfulness results in spiritual death and separation from the loving Father. (James 1:14,15, 1 John 5:17)

But our sinfulness need not become a continual way of life. We know that Christ forgives our sinfulness. Scriptures of encouragement and of interest on this point are:

- Hebrews 8:12 is a blessing within itself. Read it and see.
- 1 John 1:7-9
- Revelation 1:5
- Matthew 26:28
- Romans 4:7,8
- Hebrews 10:2,17,18
- Isaiah 44:21,22
- Psalms 103:12

All of the Scriptures are encouragers.

To the Child. Sin doesn't disappear forever. It tries to mislead us into willingly doing wrong deeds so we won't want to be close to God. Sin makes us feel unworthy of God in our lives. God hates sin and wants us to do the right thing. We can only do the right thing by believing in Jesus and trying to live like Him.

Why Did Jesus Have to Die?

To the Adult. As I sit here trying to think of the words to share with you about why Jesus Christ had to die it is very early in the morning. All night long I have tossed and turned considering this question. It is now four a.m. and the time has come to deal with this thoughtful question.

I am sure we are deeply loved by God. You see, my friend, even before we were born God assumed responsibility for keeping us safe. It is not God's will that we perish (die spiritually or physically) because of our sinful desires. God wants us to be free from the slavery that sin causes. God showed His will to care for mankind even before man and woman were created. Reread Genesis and see what God provided for Adam and Eve (all they needed).

Because sin is an act of disobedience against God it is impossible to maintain a right attitude when we sin. When we sin we are under Satan's domination, not God's. In Romans 3:19 the truth shared with us by Paul tells us that the entire human race is guilty before God and we are under condemnation of His broken laws. Only Christ lived a sinless life! Sin places us in bondage to Satan.

As a penalty for the offense of sin, it is impossible for us to redeem ourselves from sin. All our good works, all our efforts, all our tears won't get us back into fellowship with God. But we are not without hope. Here's the good news. Our human nature can be changed. Let's look at 2 Corinthians 15-19 (NAS), *"And He died for all, that they who live should no longer live for themselves, but for Him who died and rose again on their behalf. Therefore from now on we recognize no man according to the flesh; even though we have known Him thus no longer. Therefore if any man is in Christ, he is a new creature; the old things passed away; behold, new things have come. Now all these things are from God, who reconciled us to Himself through Christ, and gave us the ministry of reconciliation, namely, that God was in Christ reconciling the world to Himself, not counting their trespasses against them, and He has committed to us the word of reconciliation."*

Now that we've opened the door of truth let us walk into the light filled room and absorb the light of the living Lord with these words, *"And being found in appearance as a man, He humbled Himself and became obedient to the point of death, even the death of the cross."* Philippians 2:7,8 (NKJV)

We can go on and on with Scriptures which will enlighten us as to our need for Christ. Here is a sampling of some passages to read concerning our sinfulness and why Christ had to die:

- Isaiah 64:6
- Jeremiah 17:9
- Isaiah 1:5,6
- Ecclesiastes 7:20

Recall that repentance is obtained through Christ. Within our own power we cannot obtain it. That is why Christ died! Repentance is accepting the gift of Christ—total and complete love and forgiveness. Christ is our atonement for sin. To refuse Christ's perfect sacrifice, and the giving of His life on that terrible cross, is to say "no" to God.

Verses which will give you more insight into discovering the truth of God on this matter of why Christ died are:

- Romans 5:6
- 1 John 4:10
- 1 Peter 2:24
- Matthew 26:28
- John 1:29

There are numerous verses which will aid you in your study. Bear in mind it will take effort on your part to dig them out. But as you search the Word for truth, things grow clearer and you grow wiser.

To the Child. You might want to say, (child's name), I have been reading about sin in my Bible. Let me show you something exciting that Jesus did for us concerning sin. Jesus gave us a special gift when He took all our sins to the cross and died for us. When He did this, Jesus was saying, "I want you (child's name) to be forgiven of all wrongdoing and sin. I want you to know my Father God and believe that my gift makes a difference in your life."

The Cross

To the Adult. When I truly contemplate Jesus' death upon the cross chills run up my spine. I feel thankful for Jesus Christ. The cross, was, of course, a death that was most undesirable by the people of that day. And yet, Jesus Christ, our Lord and Savior, gave His life for you and me. Consider the humility of hanging naked upon a cross to be scorned and ridiculed. What a humbling experience it would have been for any person to die with such humiliation. Jesus endured suffering and shame with honor and dignity so that we could receive God's gift of grace.

How painful it must have been to have nails driven through His body. Talk about suffering! The wooden cross, rugged, filled with splinters, splattered with the precious blood of Jesus Christ, was supposed to be the ultimate symbol of shame. But Jesus gave the cross dignity through His sacrifice.

When our Lord submitted to death on the cross He overpowered the effectiveness of Satan. Satan could not snuff out the grace of God by killing the Lamb of God. God's perfect plan was completed through Jesus Christ's sacrifice. While Satan thought he had finally won the battle and that all of mankind would fall into his evil plan, God proved him wrong.

All the forces of evil (and don't overlook that fact) had lashed out at Jesus as He hung on the cross. Every evil thing Satan could do was thrust upon our Savior. Nothing was held back. The Son of God was subjected to the most intense misery known to mankind. Satan pulled out all the stops and yet ... he underestimated God and His wisdom.

As the hours went by the small flaw in Satan's plan was revealed. The Savior was subjected, over and over again, to the wrath of sin and evil. The small flaw became a large crack and

Satan's plan was falling apart. What an awesome feeling for the disciples and believers, like a nightmare you wish you could wake up from. My how their hearts must have grieved as they witnessed the horror of the crucifixion. But Satan's plan to overtake mankind had failed.

Had Satan won the battle at the cross we would be without any hope for eternal life. But He did not! The cross, Christ's death and resurrection, rendered Satan powerless to overcome God. Christ rescued us at the cross through His crucifixion. This was done by the fact that Satan had no power to keep Christ in the grave. We know that in three days Christ rose from the grave and the full victory was realized for those who bear the name of Christians.

To the Child. Satan had expected that the death of Jesus would put an end to goodness. But God had another plan and the cross became a symbol of victory for the Christian. God was pleased with Jesus. Jesus was willing to take the sins of the world to the cross. No one but Jesus can give eternal life, God's gift for those who will believe in Jesus as Savior and Lord.

God made Satan's plan fail. Satan has no claim to Christians because we belong to Jesus Christ. Jesus made Satan and his evil doings take second place in the world. We who live for Jesus do not have to be fearful of Satan because a part of God lives within us. All this happened and when you believe Jesus did these things for you then your heart will want to be more like Jesus in actions and deeds.

Jesus' Willingness

To the Adult. When you discuss all of these ideas with your children it is necessary to teach them that Christ was willing to follow God's plan. Christ prayed. He knew what would happen and He was ready to face up to it. He knew that if He failed then you and I would never see God. Jesus kept on praying for God's strength and courage. Jesus' prayers made Him ready for what was to come because He listened to His Father God.

His acceptance of God's will was evident. Christ's attitude and feelings were much like yours and mine. The major difference was that Christ never turned down God's requests. In the Garden of Gethsemane, the night before He was killed, Jesus prayed and asked His Father that if it were possible to find another way to redeem the human race to please do so. (Matthew 26:39) But, yet, Christ also expressed the desire that if dying was the only way to salvage mankind then He was willing.

We know, of course, that God reassured Christ. When Christ atoned for all the guilt of the world it must have been an awesome feeling. The suffering love of God bearing the guilt of mankind, placed on a cross, was a willing and loving act of submission by our Lord.

To the Child. Please remember that Jesus did what God asked of Him, always. He was willing to follow God's instructions and commands at any cost.

Additional Discussion

It is some two hours later than when I began to share my thoughts with you concerning Christ's gift to us. I am drained. In my heart there is a sense of wonder and amazement at what our Savior has done for us. Sometimes, I wonder, do we really grasp the importance of what Christ has done for us personally?

In Isaiah 1:19 the verse begins, *"Come now, and let us reason together, saith the Lord."* As you reason with Christ concerning the gift of life consider more than the facts as stated in the Scriptures. Consider what difference Christ makes in your life and how you lived before you knew Him. Think about how you might share these thoughts with your children.

For some of us it may be necessary to ask, *"Has it made a difference knowing Christ as Lord and Savior? Have I truly understood the message of Jesus Christ? Have I been willing to follow the Lord God as I know I should? Just how important is it that Christ's gift be displayed in my life?"*

These are questions that only you can answer. It is not for me to tell you where you are in your Christian walk and in your relationship with the Savior. But if you feel something is missing, something not quite right, consider Christ. Truly dwell on Him in your mind. Open your heart and ask Him to reveal Himself to you completely. Ask that He might show you all you need to know in order to share the love of God completely with your youngster.

When I consider my Lord, my heart is overwhelmed with love. He cares! He loves! He is a living, concerned Lord and Savior! Christ considered me important enough to die for me! Christ wants me to have eternal life (salvation) through Him. My heart is glad. Today, as I watch the early morning sun rise, I know to whom I belong and am glad. Christ has set me free! Praise God that He gave us a Savior.

Was Jesus Christ
Given a Fair Trial?

To the Adult. I think not! In Matthew 26:1-5 a plot is formed and agreed upon by the chief of the priests, the elders of the court and the high priest named Caiaphas. They plotted to have our Lord seized and killed.

And further on in Matthew 26:47-68 the rest of the story unfolds. Let's look at the action of the betrayal and arrest.

1. *In verse 47-56 Judas approaches Jesus and gives a kiss of betrayal.* The soldiers swarm Jesus to overpower Him. Jesus does not resist but goes with them to fulfill the will of God so that we can receive God's gift of salvation.

2. *Verses 57-68, Jesus is taken before Caiaphas, the high priest, where the scribes, elders and others are gathered.* The chief priests

and the council press their efforts to obtain false testimony against Jesus so they will have reason to put Jesus to death.

Jesus does not aid their cause and for the most part is silent before them. Then the question is asked, *"Tell us whether You are the Christ, the Son of God."*

The trap has been sprung and Jesus replies in truth, *"You have said it yourself; nevertheless I tell you, hereafter you shall see the Son of Man sitting at the right hand of Power, and coming on the clouds of heaven."* (verse 64 NAS)

The high priest, so concerned and upset at this thought, tore his robes. No doubt he shouted his reply, *"You have blasphemed! What further need do we have of witnesses?"* (verse 65b NAS)

His anger lashed out at our Savior as he spat in His face and beat Him with his fists. Others soon joined in to express their anger and resentment of Christ's words of truth.

To the Child. The people were misled by wrong thoughts and sinful attitudes. Though it was not fair, He was willing to see God's plan through. You and I should know that Jesus gave us a special gift when He took our sins to the cross. When we really believe that Jesus did this and that God forgives us then we should ask Jesus to live in our hearts. Jesus showed us that He could overcome evil through God's power and that His way was best. Let's see what else happened when Jesus was crucified.

Jesus Before Pilate

To the Adult. Now that there was a superficial reason they could use to justify their desire to kill Jesus Christ, the priests took Him before Pilate. Pilate was, as you know, the governor of the area. I expect he was less than overjoyed to be disturbed by a matter of this sort.

Pilate listened to the angry men spout their words of hate and fear. Surely, he thought, I can get out of this matter with little effort. When Pilate inquired of the people what they would have done, he was astonished. They wanted Christ to be crucified!

Pilate clearly stated his position. He saw no reason for Christ to be crucified.

Perhaps Pilate thought the anger would fade away as he mentioned the custom of releasing a prisoner during the holy festival. Surely, he thought, they would choose Jesus as the one to be freed. With shaky confidence he might have asked, "Would you have me release Barabas, the notorious, hate-filled, prisoner or do you prefer the release of this man who claims to be the Son of God?"

Don't you imagine that Pilate felt remorse when the people cried out, "Crucify Jesus! Crucify Jesus!"? Pilate washed his hands of the blood of Jesus and told them to do what they wished.

A fair trial? Not at all! Consider how you would feel if you were given a trial of this sort. I am sure you would have felt mistreated and desired a new trial. Jesus was treated unfairly! To say the very least it was shabby justice. The evil of man's old nature (to have its way at any cost) prevailed at Jesus' trial.

Jesus wasn't given a chance. The plot to kill Jesus was a success. But as we will see, death did not bind our Lord Jesus Christ in the grave forever.

To the Child. Pilate knew the people were wrong. He tried to change their minds but could not. They had become puppets of Satan's plan.

The Resurrection of Jesus Christ

To the Adult. Why is it important that we relate the full story of Jesus Christ's death, burial and resurrection to our children? Simply because the story of eternal life through Jesus Christ is not complete until all the facts are known.

Reading John 19 can enlighten us concerning the importance of knowing what happened to Jesus before, during and after the crucifixion. Why not take a few moments and look at two chapters which are vital in sharing the "good news" with your young person. Were it not for John 19 and 20 many of our questions would remain unanswered concerning the "whys" of this important event.

Recall that the soldiers were going to break the legs of Jesus and the two crucified with Him so they would die and be taken down before the Sabbath. It seems cruel to us but to the soldiers it was expedient. When they came to Jesus they saw that He was already dead. The soldiers pierced the side of Christ with a spear (v.34) and blood and water came forth. This was a sure sign to the soliders, who had witnessed many of these horrible deaths, that the victim was dead. They saw no need to break the legs of Christ and thus He was removed from the cross.

This also was a fulfillment of the Scripture, *"Not a bone of Him shall be broken."* And again another Scripture says, *"They shall look on Him whom they pierced."* (verses 36c,37 NAS)

Joseph of Arimathea, a wealthy man and a follower of the Lord, asked Pilate for permission to take the body of Christ and place it in a tomb for burial. Pilate quickly gave approval.

To the Child. Jesus died on the cross and was placed in a tomb for burial. But Jesus' spirit overcame death and lives on. Christians will live on forever. And as our spirits are renewed we will be in the presence of the Lord forever and forever!

The Body Prepared for Burial

To the Adult. There was no doubt that Christ was dead, as Nicodemus and Joseph prepared the body for burial. Using a mixture of myrrh and aloes they cared for the Master's body. Then they took linen wrappings and spices and bound the body, as was the Jewish custom. (See verses 38-40)

The natural body of Jesus Christ was enclosed in a new tomb. There is no doubt that the tomb was sealed tight by the soldiers. Jesus' body lay in the tomb for three days. His spirit was separated from His body.

Mary Magdalene and Mary (the other Mary) were sitting opposite the grave. (Matthew 27:61)

He Is Risen!

Matthew 28 recalls the event, *"Now after the Sabbath, as it began to dawn toward the first day of the week, Mary Magdalene and the other Mary came to look at the grave. And behold, a severe earthquake had occurred, for an angel of the Lord descended from heaven and came and rolled away the stone and sat upon it. And his appearance was like lightning, and his garment as white as snow; and the guards shook for fear of him, and became like dead men. And the angel answered and said to the women, 'Do not be afraid; for I know that you are looking for Jesus who has been crucified. He is not here, for He has risen, just as He said. Come, see the place where He was lying.'"* (verses 1-6 NAS)

What encouragement the women must have felt as they saw that Christ was gone. He had done the things He promised. He had risen from the grave and defeated the hold death had on the spirit. How wonderful! Christ was alive! Christ still is alive! Be glad and share this good word with your children.

Because Christ arose from the grave and ascended into heaven, we know that we who believe in Him have the same reward, a place with the Father. You see Jesus keeps His promises. Jesus ascended into heaven to be with the Father and to prepare a place for Christians to dwell with Him when we leave this earth. *Wow!*

To the Child. I hope you understand how important it was for Jesus to live, die on the cross, and rise from the grave. You see, there was nothing any power or any person could do to keep Jesus in the grave. Jesus showed us that His gift to us, eternal life, gives new life. When we become Christians and try to live like Jesus taught us, then we have something to be very glad about.

Jesus showed us that evil could not keep Him from obeying God. We should remember that evil has no place in our lives. We want to have a good and happy life and that life is found in following Jesus Christ.

Jesus After
The Resurrection

To the Adult. Over a period of time after His resurrection, Jesus appeared several times in numerous places. Were He not God this would have been impossible. We have discussed the fact that Jesus is a part of the Trinity with our children. Therefore, we know that nothing Christ did was impossible. Our children should also be reminded that Satan couldn't stop Jesus from making God's plan work. He reassured His followers and the disciples that He was the One promised by God. (John 20:19-29) Read the account for yourself so that you might better understand the events of the moment.

Jesus appeared at the Sea of Galilee and what happened? Read John 21:1-15 and see. Don't skip over it for this example will clearly demonstrate how Jesus provides for His own. I consider this an important example of Jesus' continued concern for His followers.

During these last days of Jesus' earthly visit the disciples received instruction and information. Christ made many interesting statements. Let's look at John 20:19-23 (NAS) and read these words of encouragement together: "When therefore it was evening, on that day, the first day of the week, and when the doors were shut where the disciples were, for fear of the Jews, Jesus came and stood in their midst, and said to them, 'Peace be with you.' And when He had said this, He showed them both His hands and His side. The disciples therefore rejoiced when they saw the Lord. Jesus therefore said to them again, 'Peace be with you; as the Father has sent Me, I also send you.' "

"And when He had said this, He breathed on them, and said to them, 'Receive the Holy Spirit. If you forgive the sins of any, their sins have been forgiven them; if you retain the sins of any, they have been retained.' "

No matter what you discuss with your children be sure your words always show God's concern for mankind. Jesus used His words to encourage those who believed in Him. Likewise, we should experience the same source of encouragement as we read the Scriptures.

To the Child. As proof that Jesus lives forever, He made many visits among the people. During this time Jesus continued to teach and direct people toward God.

Final Appearance to the Apostles

To the Adult: "Afterward he appeared to the eleven as they sat at the table; and He rebuked their unbelief and hardness of heart, because they believed not those who had seen Him after He had risen. And He said to them, 'Go into all the world, and preach the gospel to every creature. He who believes and is baptized will be saved; but he who does not believe will be condemned. And these signs will follow those who believe: In My name they will cast out demons; they will speak with new tongues; they will take up serpents; and if they drink anything deadly, it will by no means hurt them; they will lay hands on the sick, and they will recover.' So then, after the Lord had spoken to them, he was received up into heaven, and sat down at the right hand of God. And they went out and preached everywhere, the Lord working with them and confirming the word through the accompanying signs. Amen."
Mark 16:14-20 (NKJV)

What words of encouragement! Jesus keeps His promises. He did and still does the things He has said He would do. We live in some shaky times and as each day passes our children need to have the security of Jesus Christ in their lives. What better gift to share with our children than the full knowledge of Jesus Christ as our Lord and Savior.

To the Child. Never forget that Jesus offered you a special gift. He did something you and I couldn't do—He made it possible for us to enter the family of God. There is no other way to belong to God than to accept the gift of grace offered to you by Jesus Christ. If you believe that Jesus is Savior and died for you then you can receive eternal life. If you want to live with God from this day on then ask Jesus to be your Lord and Savior. Jesus Christ will show you that a life filled with God is the best life of all.

You have an opportunity to come to Jesus, as a young person, and explore the goodness of God all the days of your life. The Bible is the guidebook of faith for all Christians. Ask for help in understanding and reading it. Then ask Jesus to open your eyes to the greatest gift of all—God's love as offered through His Son Jesus Christ.

chapter six

Accepting Jesus' Gift

This chapter centers on the very heart of Christianity, eternal life, salvation, and new birth through Jesus Christ. Before you run and hide because you aren't sure you know how to discuss this with your child, consider this:

- You are your child's most effective witness regarding faith in Christ.
- Your child knows you better than anyone else.
- Who better than you can help your child come to fully understand Jesus Christ?
- What is the greatest blessing you have received from Christ?
- Don't you want this blessing to be your child's too?

Have Faith and Believe in God

To the Adult. Faith is something that is learned each day. It does not come in an instant. It comes by experiencing God's faithfulness and learning to trust God. Faith is gained by hearing, studying and then applying the information learned to our individual lives.

The first thing children should learn is that God is faithful. He does the things He says He will do. God never goes back on His word but stands firm and true. God is constant and never changing. He is just and righteous to those who need punishment. Those who merit reward for their deeds and actions will receive it from God so that God may be glorified through their Christian walk.

"Now faith is the assurance of the things we hope for, the proof of the reality of the things we cannot see. For by it the men of old won God's approval. By faith we understand that the worlds were created, beautifully co-ordinated, and now exist, at God's command; so the things that we see did not develop out of mere matter." Hebrews 11:1-3 (Williams)

These passages, perhaps some of the most widely quoted, explain faith. Let's examine these passages closely to determine what we might say in speaking of faith to a child.

- "the reality of things we cannot see":

What are some of the things we cannot see? There are many. We cannot see the wind but we know it is there. We see it rustle the leaves in the trees. We are aware of the wind blowing storms across the land. We watch as a kite rises and soars in the brisk March breeze. While we do not see the wind we know it is there. We are confident that the wind will remain with us and function properly. You will recall God is a spirit and spirits are not seen with the visible eye. He can be anywhere at any moment in time. God is not bound by limitations and can move as the wind anywhere He pleases.

You see, the comparison of the wind and God allows the child to think of God in a real manner. Both the wind and God are real but none of us can see either of them. (This would be a great time to mention that God created the wind. Always reaffirm God as creator of the universe as you talk to your youngster. When we do this we will build our child's security and faith for each new day.)

- "By faith we understand the worlds were created"

The Scriptures certainly say more than a mouthful in these three verses. Learning to believe in God comes only through faith. We have to believe that God is and does the things the Bible tells us He does. We have to allow our faith to open up and function freely, unhampered by distrust and skepticism.

We are a people who are almost intent on making God fit our mold of Him. God created the worlds, the stars, the universe, and God created us. As part of God's creation we must conform to God's standards and His will. The one created is not greater than the Creator. The person who tries to make God fit their mold is a fool. Allow them to understand and see that God is real to you and that you are grateful for the mighty work of God among us. Help your youngsters understand that God has blessed us in many ways and wants us to know all about Him.

It seems we understand so very little concerning faith and what it does. Faith is mentioned as childlike. It is my opinion that adults are prone to stumble over God because they won't allow their natural faith to function freely. We don't want God to be God. We try to change Him, alter His plans and make Him a god of convenience. Faith, when allowed to work in a normal and healthy manner, allows us to enjoy experiencing God's maximum love toward us.

Children really do want to trust and believe in something or someone. Your opportunities to share your faith in God with your child are limitless. This little child whom you have loved, comforted, guided and cared for looks up to you for answers. As you speak, lovingly, about God the child will gain trust and confidence and develop his or her own faith. Your youngsters know you are not in the habit of misleading them, so surely the things you say about God are true.

Faith is a living example of belief in action. Faith is discussed in greater detail in Chapter 10.

To the Child. Faith is something you learn daily. It is learning to trust Jesus in all areas of your life. After you begin to trust Jesus you will notice how much He helps you. The more you believe He is your helper and guide the more He will be able to do for you.

Sharing Christ

To the Adult. There are a variety of ways to share Christ with children and adults. Some people like to scare others into salvation and use the shock approach. Still others use a planned methodical approach. Many Christians use the gentle method of discussing Christ and salvation. Since I am a mild mannered person and disapprove of the shock approach, gentleness wins out.

Scaring anyone to believe in and trust in the Lord Jesus Christ seems drastic to me. Besides, it isn't really fair! I realize some feel an effective method of bringing others to Christ is the fright and shock method but still I consider love the best approach. Christ is our example and He used love to bring others to a full knowledge that He was the promised Savior of mankind.

We have discussed how mankind's sinful nature resulted from the disobedience in the Garden of Eden. When your children realize that they are sinful by nature they must begin to deal with it. There is no legitimate reason for us to tell children over and over again they are sinful creatures. This only confuses them and often times upsets sensitive children to the point where they find it difficult to cope with their need to make a decision. You know, we can be told something so often that the negative gains our focus. We can, in fact, feel that because of our old sinful attitudes we are not worthy to be "saved" or receive the gift of "eternal life." (My point—Don't dwell on sinfulness and negative issues in discussing the gift of salvation through Jesus Christ.)

To the Child. Each of us should be glad to share our faith in Jesus. When we share our love for Jesus, others will want to know more about Him.

Why Jesus Came

To the Adult. You should desire to gain as much insight as possible concerning salvation and believing in Christ before talking to your child. This is an important topic and you will want to find a quiet place to discuss eternal things. Speak to your child in loving terms about Christ. Allow him or her to ask questions as you supply information concerning God's perfect love as displayed in the life of Jesus Christ.

To the Child. Now let's consider some important facts we have learned concerning God and mankind:

- Man and woman were originally endowed with God's greatest gifts.

They had everything they needed but they wanted the one thing God told them was not good to have.

- Selfishness, weakness, and self-centered attitudes were able to seize control of Adam and Eve.

They were tempted by the serpent, who was Satan in disguise, and committed sin. They did wrong according to the rules God had set for them. Adam and Eve were lured into seeking their own goals and forgetting about God's desires for their lives.

- The peace and harmony Adam and Eve had experienced quickly departed their lives, replaced by an attitude and feeling of guilt.
- Adam and Eve lied to God about what they had done.

Satan's lie to Eve led to sin, then another lie was necessary to cover the first sin. On and on it would continue. Sin had to be punished.

- God had to punish Adam and Eve for their sinful attitudes.

He made them leave the garden. They no longer lived in perfect peace with God. They had to toil and labor to provide for their needs.

- Likewise, we know that it is impossible for us, because of our old human nature, to escape from sin.

Our human nature causes us to fall into sin time and time again.

- Sin (wrongdoing) keeps us from experiencing full fellowship and the total love of God.
- Throughout history mankind has struggled with sin, despair, anguish, suffering, and hardship.

The more we want the things that are not good for us, the worse things seem to become.

- God wanted us to have restored fellowship with Him.

That is why Jesus came.

To the Child. Since Adam and Eve first sinned in the Garden of Eden, that sin has caused mankind to be separated from God. That means we couldn't have a close relationship with Him. Jesus, through His life and sacrifice, has made it possible for Christians to be close to God again. Jesus really did something special for us. I want you to know that I am glad He died so you and I could have eternal life.

Why Should
Your Child Believe?

To the Adult. Without the blessing of salvation there are only shallow moments of happiness. Time and time again people refuse Christ and sink back into hopeless situations. Sin darkens the life of the unbeliever and blinds spiritual vision. Finally, and sadly, the person refuses to see God's goodness at all and the spiritual darkness lingers on.

Isn't it sad to think that children would never find the light of the Lord because they were never told about Christ? As adults we have a responsibility to share the "good news" with our young friends and family members. We want no one to live without knowing about our Lord Jesus Christ.

Why believe? John 3 gives us many of the answers. Turn with me to the book of John and read along. John 3:3 KJV, *"Jesus answered, and said unto him, 'Verily, verily, I say unto thee, except a man be born again, he cannot see the kingdom of God.'"*

Unless we accept God's free gift of salvation, we will not see the kingdom of God. The only way to be a part of the kingdom of God is through acceptance of Jesus Christ as Lord and Savior.

To the Child. God wants the best for us and that is why He sent Jesus to earth to tell about the love of God offered to all who will accept it.

"For God so loved the world that He gave His only begotten Son, that who ever believes in Him should not perish but have everlasting life." John 3:16 (NKJV)

Jesus Came
to Save, Not Condemn

To the Adult. God's only Son, Jesus Christ, saves us from perishing. God gave His son as a sacrifice for our sinfulness. Make sure your young person understands God is a very personal God. His work is done one to one. The following Scripture states this truth clearly.

"For God did not send His Son into the world to condemn the world, but that the world though Him might be saved. He that believes in Him is not condemned; but He who does not believe is condemned already, because he has not believed in the name of the only begotten Son of God." John 3:17,18 (NKJV)

There is a tremendous amount of truth in these two verses. Help your youngster understand that nothing in the world can buy the love of God. The person who believes in Jesus is not condemned but is free to experience the joy of the Christ-like life. Those who do not or will not believe in the name of God's only Son are without hope both now and throughout eternity.

You might want to explain eternity at this point. Although it seems difficult to comprehend, God tells us that eternity goes on and on and on. For example, you might want to say something similar to the following as you talk with your child.

To the Child. "Can you imagine (child's name) being with God forever and forever? Won't it be wonderful to see all the things God has for us and to be happy forever? No tears, no pain, no suffering when we spend eternity with God. That's great! Well, (child's name), when you know Jesus as the one who died for your sins and ask Jesus to be a part of your life then God gives you a special gift called eternal life (or salvation). To be a Christian means you want to live in the Family of God."

Repentance

To the Adult. When we desire to set our lives on a new course and follow Christ, what do we do? Step one . . . we repent. Repent means to change our attitudes and ways. Repentance is turning away from sin in our lives. In Matthew 11:28 Jesus calls us to come to Him. His plea is issued to the burdened and to those who are in distress and seek inner rest. Don't be deceived into thinking your child does not experience heavy burdens of some sort. Their burdens may be insignificant to you but to your child they are very real.

When you discuss repentance talk about it as a turning away from those ugly and useless things that cause us to do something we *know* to be wrong.

To the Child. Even though the word "repent" sounds awful, it isn't. When we repent we are saying we want to try and be more like Jesus and we know that is *good*.

Confession

To the Adult. There are many things to cover in considering the blessings and joys of believing. Remember as we study this area that we are encouragers as well as enlighteners as we share our faith. We will use a wide assortment of Scriptures. You will find some which speak to you in a special manner. Others may not be as meaningful but all are of equal importance.

"If we confess our sins, he is faithful and just to forgive us our sins and to cleanse us from all unrighteousness." 1 John 1:9 (NKJV)

As young people accept Christ as Savior and realize that sin displeases God they will more than likely desire to set their lives back on the right track. Confession that they have done wrong (sinned) is the first step. Sin has to be admitted before it can be dealt with. It isn't always easy to say, "I have done something wrong." But to receive forgiveness from God our mistakes have to be aired and we have to want to change our ways. It isn't easy but it is God's way. We don't have to be overly fearful that God will punish us, for we have the gift of grace.

You see, Christ liberated us from sin's condemnation. (John

3:18) Our claim to God's grace and mercy is acquired through Jesus. Reread 1 John 1:9. When your children understand that God is waiting to forgive wrongs and forget them they will be more receptive to God's gift of grace. None of us wants to be punished, and knowing that Christ has paid our debt should give us added joy because we know Christ.

To the Child. When we do wrong we need to say so; admit it. God knows our hearts and when we say we are sorry, He understands. We have to say I'm sorry to God when we do wrong. God forgives us because Jesus died on the cross for our sins.

It is important to confess our sins. You see, He is faithful and just to do what? To forgive and cleanse us from all unrighteousness. Examine this truth . . . Assurance of salvation is gained by knowing the positive things that God has given us through the Scriptures. Positive teachings will quench doubts.

Believe: Have Faith

To the Adult. As the conscience of your child moves toward the need for and belief in Christ as Savior, be an encourager. Help your child realize that believing in Christ is simple. To believe in Jesus is to understand that He gave Himself for you and your sins. When your child understands and believes the promises of Christ, he or she will know: (1) that we are forgiven of our sins through Jesus; (2) that we are cleansed (refreshed and made whole through Christ); and (3) we have new life through Christ's gift of salvation (eternal life). Then your young person can begin to experience the blessings of God's grace.

Your children don't have to wait to feel forgiven or cleansed from their sins before they accept Christ's gift. I doubt they would ever accept His gift if they waited until they felt cleansed. But realizing that you belong to Christ and are forgiven a decision shouldn't be far off. There is no condemnation to those in Jesus Christ. Romans 8 is a perfect example of the new life Christ gives.

Read it with your children. Help them secure their beliefs by hearing the Word of God and applying it to their lives.

To the Child. To believe in Jesus and have faith is to say you trust Him like you do your mom and dad. Jesus will never let you down. Jesus will always be your friend. Jesus loves you very much.

Giving Your Life to Jesus

To the Adult. Becoming a Chistian means just that—giving your life to Jesus. Your children should find pleasure in learning that once they have given their lives to Jesus they are adopted children of God. Isn't that a great gift? And it's true!

Believing is your child's personal commitment to Christ. Giving your life to Jesus means you want to claim the promises and gifts that God has set aside for those who belong in the Family of God. Even greater blessings come from experiencing God's love.

Scriptures That Will
Help You Discuss Christ

"Therefore if any man is in Christ, he is a new creature; the old things passed away; behold, new things have come." 2 Corinthians 5:17 (NAS)

Life takes on new meaning when you belong to Christ. With a growing knowledge of Christ we gain new knowledge and a different perspective on life. Christ begins to teach your children what is important in life. As your children learn what is important in their Christian lives they realize they are free to choose their own course. They begin to understand that their peers don't always make the right choices. Now they see "doing your own thing" is not always right. Christ allows them to view life with new eyes, eyes opened by the light of Christ.

"Truly, truly, I say to you, he who hears My word, and believes Him who sent Me, has eternal life, and does not come into judgment but has passed out of death into life." John 5:24 (NAS)

"Draw near to God and He will draw near to you. Cleanse your hands, you sinners; and purify your hearts, you double-minded." James 4:8 (NAS)

"Behold, I stand at the door and knock; if any one hears My voice and opens the door, I will come in to him, and will dine with him, and he with Me." Revelation 3:20 (NAS)

"All that the Father gives Me shall come to Me, and the one who comes to Me I will certainly not cast out." John 6:37 (NAS)

Other verses of value in discussing your child's decision to follow Christ are listed below. Since our space is limited these Scriptures are listed for your convenience as you research them for yourself.

- 1 John 3:1-17
- Galatians 3:7,26
- John 1:12,13
- John 3:1-11
- Romans 4:16,17
- Matthew 26:28
- Romans 10:9-19
- Romans 5:6-10
- Acts 16:31
- Isaiah 53:5,6
- Romans 10:13

"But who ever keeps His word, truly the love of God is perfected in him. By this we know that we are in Him. He who says he abides in Him ought himself also to walk just as He walked." 1 John 2:5,6 (NKJV)

When you believe in Christ you can grow in faith and become a little more like Jesus. Your young person will begin to desire a lifestyle which experiences love, concern, tenderness, a caring attitude, and sensitivity. Your child can dare to be different because Christ lives within.

We could go on and on but cannot for there is much ground to cover as we share with our young persons. (Note: Scriptures are to be used as our chief source of strength and encouragement. It is through the Scriptures that understanding and knowledge of God is found. Use your Bible as often as possible in discussing your faith with your child.)

To the Child. When you believe in Jesus and accept His gift of salvation God adopts you into His Family. Because you have faith in Jesus, believe that He died for your sins, and openly say so—you are a Christian. If you want to do this here is a prayer for us to pray together.

Dear God,

I believe Jesus died for my wrongdoings and sin. I ask You to forgive my mistakes. I have trusted in Jesus and want to be like Him. Thank You, God, for Jesus' special gift to me of eternal life. Thank You for Your love and grace as offered to me through Your Son Jesus Christ. Amen.

Now that your young person believes in Christ and has decided to follow Him there is more to learn. You see, parent, grandparent, friend, aunt, uncle or Sunday School teacher, the learning process has just begun.

Chapter Summary

Christians believe that Christ came and bore our sins on the cross at Calvary. Only Christ sets us free from sin. Read Hebrews 9:12 and it will help you understand that through the blood of Christ we have obtained eternal redemption.

Christ's death atoned for our sin. At the cross of Calvary, He took our place before God to receive the agony, pain, torment, personal shame, and full consequences of bearing our guilt and sin. Consider this thought fully! Christ bore the punishment for all our sins in order that we might know and experience God. Because our Lord and Savior stood in our place, we can and do have fellowship with God. We are forgiven through Christ's atoning sacrifice.

Faith is learning to trust and believe the truths we have studied. With this we understand that God has provided a way for us to be His children throughout eternity. Only by accepting the atonement Christ made for us will salvation come. It isn't anything you and I have done but what Jesus Christ has done that allows us to receive salvation. God's gift to us, "new life," comes through Jesus Christ.

It can stagger our minds and should stir our hearts as we consider the full impact of salvation. Just to know that God cared enough to redeem us from sin is a mindboggler. That is why we must learn to walk by faith instead of sight. God welcomes us with open arms and invites us into the family of God as we receive salvation through Christ the Lord and our Savior.

chapter seven

The Holy Spirit

Each time we share the wonder of God it seems there is something even more exciting to learn. This chapter is special. I have looked forward to sharing it with you for some time.

Introduction

To the Adult. The Holy Spirit's function is invaluable in our spiritual growth. When we comprehend that the Holy Spirit is living within us then we should view our lives as worthwhile and valuable. It is the Holy Spirit who enables us to understand the mysteries of life. He lends us the strength and courage we need as we encounter the adversaries of spiritual darkness and evil. This same Spirit encourages, teaches, and directs us. He reveals the wisdom and knowledge of God to us because we belong to Christ.

God provided our needs not only through Christ but through the third part of the Trinity, the Holy Spirit. Each day can be thrilling as we experience the joy of being filled with the Holy Spirit working in our lives. For the Christians who do not understand the role and function of the Spirit there may be moments of great dissatisfaction and discouragement as they seek to live a balanced lifestyle. You see, they have not fully understood the Holy Spirit as a teacher, helper and guide. Do you know that many Christians experience salvation and yet miss the blessings of the abundant life? The abundant life is lived with full knowledge of God in our lives and allowing that Spirit to perform God's work through us.

Before beginning our discussion concerning the Holy Spirit let's look at some important facts about Him.

1. The Holy Spirit helps us learn Godly joy.
2. He is the source of the abundant life. (The life that overflows through a personal relationship with God our Father.) The Holy Spirit reveals God to each of us according to God's plan for our individual challenges.
3. The Holy Spirit glorifies Christ by furthering the mission of Christ. Christians filled with the Holy Spirit are also filled with the Spirit of Jesus Christ. The Holy Spirit helps us to display our personal commitment to Christ the Lord. He does, indeed, testify that Christ is in us. (John 15:26)
4. Christ informed the disciples that the Spirit would come to aid and comfort them after His death. He issued a command to receive this Spirit and go forth in the name of Jesus Christ our Lord and Savior to serve God.
5. The Holy Spirit intercedes on our behalf. (Romans 8:26) He stands as our representative before the Father and acknowledges that we are, indeed, members of the Family of God. He states our case, our need, so to speak, and is on our side.
6. The Spirit leads us. (Romans 8:14)
7. He appoints. (Acts 20:28)
8. The Holy Spirit is our special guide. Without the Holy Spirit's guiding light we would quickly go astray and never explore the depths of God's love. (John 16:13)
9. He is all-powerful and eternal. (Luke 1:35, Hebrews 9:14)
10. He is everywhere at the same time. (Psalms 139:7)
11. He is all knowing. (1 Corinthians 2:10,11)

To the Child. The Holy Spirit is our special friend. He comes to each Christian as our helper and guide. You could say, "Ray, (Child's name), let me share with you some of the things I have learned about the Holy Spirit. I want you to understand more about Him." Then you might begin to share some of the basics concerning the Holy Spirit's function.

With these facts concerning the Holy Spirit in mind, let us seek to learn more about His function in the life of the Christian. While it may be difficult for us to understand some of the information, we have full confidence that God will open our hearts to the things we must know in this matter.

Who Is the Holy Spirit?

Let's begin, *"And I will ask the Father, and He will give you another Helper, that He may be with you forever, that is the Spirit of truth, whom the world cannot receive, because it does not behold Him or know Him, but you know Him because He abides with you, and will be in you. I will not leave you as orphans; I will come to you. After a little while the world will behold Me no more; but you will behold Me; because I live, you shall live also. In that day you shall know that I am in My Father, and you in Me, and I in you. He who has My commandments and keeps them, he it is who loves Me; and he who loves Me shall be loved by My Father, and I will love him, and will disclose Myself to him."* John 14:16-21 (NAS)

To the Adult and Child. The Holy Spirit has a personality. He has emotions, a will, intellect and a purpose for being. The Holy Spirit is the One sent to fill our needs after the death of Christ. The Holy Spirit is the Comforter. (John 15:26, John 16:7) The Holy Spirit has been sent from Christ. For further information on the Spirit, read chapters 14 through 16 of John's gospel with your child. As you read together help your child understand these passages.

To the Adult. The Holy Spirit has many functions. He not only convicts us of sin in our lives, but tells us that Jesus is the Chosen One (the Messiah, the Deliverer, the Righteous One) sent from God. You see, the work of the Spirit is unlimited. It is He who opens our eyes to the things of God.

The Holy Spirit reveals Jesus Christ as the way, the truth, and the life. (John 14:6) Sometimes we need help in discovering the true facts about Jesus Christ. It is the Holy Spirit who enables us to determine what is true and what is not. It is His Spirit who sheds light in the spiritual darkness. He reveals Christ as the righteous Savior of mankind. The Holy Spirit is the best teacher available to the believer.

To the Child. The Holy Spirit awakens us to the happenings around us. He opens our spiritual eyes to right and wrong. He allows us to experience God at work in our lives. He shows us that wrong doesn't need to be a part of our lives and uses Jesus as our example of how to live for God.

OUR SPIRITUAL TEACHER

"But, as the Scripture says, they are: 'Things which eye has never seen and ear has never heard, and never have occurred to human hearts, which God prepared for those who love Him.' For God unveiled them to us through His Spirit, for the Spirit by searching discovers everything, even the deepest truths about God. For what man can understand his own inner thoughts except by his own spirit within him? Just so no one but the Spirit of God can understand the thoughts of God. Now we have not received the spirit that belongs to the world but the Spirit that comes from God, that we may get an insight into the blessings God has graciously given us. These truths we are setting forth, not in words that man's wisdom teaches but in words that the Spirit teaches, in this way

fitting spiritual words to spiritual truths." 1 Corinthians 2:9-13 (Williams)

To the Adult. What a blessing it is for those who follow Christ to know that we have the most informed teacher on the subject of our faith: the Holy Spirit. Who knows more about God than God? The Holy Spirit has firsthand experience concerning God and Christ for He is the third part of the Trinity.

God wanted His people fully informed and thus the Holy Spirit was given as our spiritual guide. We don't have to wonder about or unravel the mysteries of God for the Holy Spirit, God's personal representative, teaches us individually and collectively. He teaches us in all areas of our religious training.

To the Child. Read the above Scripture passages with your child. Help him or her to understand that humans, with our limitations, are unable to understand God. Then explain that God sent His Holy Spirit to live in us and teach us individually, through the Bible, the things that God wants us to know. Be sure they understand that through the Holy Spirit, God has given each of us the ability to read and understand His Word (The Bible). We need to listen and learn from those who God sends but we also need to learn individually from Scriptures, letting the Master Teacher, the Holy Spirit teach us. It is very important to study for ourselves so we aren't misled by wrong ideas or teachings.

OUR GUIDE

To the Adult. *"But when the Spirit of truth comes, He will guide you into the whole truth; for He will not speak on His own authority but will tell what is told Him, and will announce to you the things that are to come."* John 16:13 (Williams)

Reread the passage. Take time to reflect on it and think about what it means to you. Let the Holy Spirit bring understanding to your heart and mind. Then, after you have done that, read the example below. Think about the Scripture and the example and then use it or a similar example to explain these truths to your child.

To the Child. Have you ever toured a cave? When entering the cave you may experience a feeling of uneasiness. This is strange territory and you are unfamiliar with it. Were you to explore the area on your own there would be certain danger ahead. But if a guide has been provided to show you how to view your surroundings, you can trek through this mysterious place with confidence that things will go well. The confidence you experience is real because you trust and believe your guide to show you the right way to travel. Your guide has knowledge of the area and knows where the dangerous areas are located. Someone has prepared the way for you and you are safe. Likewise, your guide points out the areas of special interest making you aware of the unique areas of the cave. Your guide's prior experience is priceless as you walk on, secure in your surroundings.

A guide is provided to lead you through the cave so that you will not fall into peril or be confronted with some unknown element which might cause you harm. Thus it is with the Holy Spirit, our Spiritual guide. He knows His work ever so well. Would God want you to wander into the unknown without the best possible guide? No, no indeed!

ENLIGHTENMENT

To the Adult. 1 Corinthians 2:10, Ephesians 4:23, 24 and Romans 12:2 are verses which speak of transforming our old lives into something new. By using biblical examples your youngster should understand the value of the "new life."

"And do not be conformed to this world, but be transformed by the renewing of your mind, that you may prove what the will of God is, that which is good and acceptable and perfect." Romans 12:2 (NAS)

"For to us God revealed them through the Spirit; for the Spirit searches all things, even the depths of God." 1 Corinthians 2:10 (NAS)

". . . be renewed in the spirit of your mind, and put on the new self, which in the likeness of God has been created in righteousness and holiness of truth." Ephesians 4:23,24 (NAS)

The Holy Spirit enlightens and reveals even the depths of God. That's good to know. As you discuss the Holy Spirit with your children it should encourage them as they understand how the Holy Spirit functions. The Holy Spirit reveals what is good and acceptable in our Christian lives. You see, it is because we believe in Christ that we "become new persons."

The Holy Spirit allows children to see attitudes and manners which need change and shows them how this is done. The Holy Spirit is a special friend and companion to each Christian. We should encourage our children to know about the Holy Spirit.

To the Child. To understand God's way Christians receive the Holy Spirit. No other faith has this special Helper because God teaches the only way to know Him is through Jesus Christ. The Holy Spirit sheds spiritual light on things which are important. He shows us where changes need to be made in our lives. He also warns us when wrong things try to fool us into doing wrong.

Discussing Scriptures
Concerning the Holy Spirit

To the Adult. In this section we are going to look at individual passages and discuss them. Read through this section, reflect on it, then share it with your children.

As we learn more about the Holy Spirit and His function the

better we will understand God. As we tune in to God and study the Scriptures it will be easier to share our insights with our children. (You know it is difficult to intelligently discuss something we have little or no personal knowledge of ourselves. But remember our youngsters are counting on us.) Discussion of Scriptures opens new doors of understanding. So then, let us journey in joy as we share from the Word of God, the Holy Bible.

Scripture

"For all who are being led by the Spirit of God, these are sons of God. For you have not received a spirit of slavery leading to fear again, but you have received a spirit of adoption as sons by which we cry out, Abba! Father! The Spirit Himself bears witness with our spirit that we are children of God, and if children, heirs also, heirs of God and fellow heirs with Christ, if indeed we suffer with Him in order that we may also be glorified with Him." Romans 8:14-17 (NAS)

It cannot be overly stated, first, that we who believe in Christ have been adopted by God. Reaffirm this belief with your child. Secondly, "led by the Spirit of God." Led by what? The Spirit Himself! What words of cheer! The Spirit is available to lead us wherever we go. No matter what situation your children encounter there is a helper, comforter and guide—the Holy Spirit.

Scripture

"However, you are not in the flesh but in the Spirit, if indeed the Spirit of God dwells in you. But if anyone does not have the Spirit of Christ, he does not belong to Him. And if Christ is in you, though the body is dead because of sin, yet the spirit is alive because of righteousness. But if the Spirit of Him who raised Jesus from the dead dwells in you, He who raised Christ Jesus from the dead will also give life to your mortal bodies through His Spirit who indwells you." Romans 8:9-11 (NAS)

These passages are easily understood, aren't they? If we have the Spirit of Christ in us shouldn't we live differently than non-believers? Yes indeed! With the Holy Spirit active in our lives we will strive to live by God's standards, not the world's (human) standards. You may want to use the following in discussing this passage with your children.

We who believe in Christ are adopted into the family of God. We belong to God because we accept Jesus Christ as our Savior. We are important to God, so important that He gives us a part of His spirit to live within us. Isn't that wonderful? Just imagine (Child's name) God's gift of grace not only gives us eternal life but a part of God lives in each Christian so we will know right from wrong.

Scriptures

"And you also were included in Christ when you heard the word of truth, the gospel of your salvation. Having believed, you were marked in him with a seal, the promised Holy Spirit, who is a deposit guaranteeing our inheritance until the redemption of those who are God's possession—to the praise of his glory." Ephesians 1:13,14 (NIV)

"And do not grieve the Holy Spirit of God, with whom you were sealed for the day of redemption." Ephesians 4:30 (NIV)

"Now it is God who makes both us and you stand firm in Christ. He anointed us, set his seal of ownership on us, and put his Spirit in our hearts as a deposit, guaranteeing what is to come." 2 Corinthians 1:21,22 (NIV)

Don't you find comfort in the thought that believers in Christ are sealed in our faith? We are protected and God has placed His stamp of ownership on us. His Spirit has placed a deposit in our hearts. With the deposit there is a guarantee of our inheritance in the Kingdom of God. Wow!

Do you see the importance of these Scriptures? The Christian life is more than believing and accepting Christ as Savior. These are only the beginning steps in our walk of faith. It is exciting to be a Christian.

The seal we receive suggests to me that we have God's personal pledge of security for each believer. We will receive a spiritual body, at Jesus Christ's return. We are guaranteed an inheritance in the Kingdom which is yet to come. We have the security of knowing the Holy Spirit is available to guide us throughout this life.

Additional Scriptures to Study

Here are some selected verses for you to share concerning the Holy Spirit. Look them up and read them for further enlightenment. Using the previous section as a guide, discuss their meaning with your children. Remember, the Holy Spirit will help you in your understanding.

- He comforts: Acts 9:31
- He directs missionaries: Acts 13:2
- He helps us in our infirmities: Romans 8:26
- The Holy Spirit dwells within us: 1 Corinthians 6:19
- He is spoken of as dwelling within the disciples: John 14:17
- He sanctifies: Hebrews 15:16, 2 Thessalonians 2:13
- Receive power through Him: 1 Corinthians 2:3-5

chapter eight

Gifts and Talents

One of the first things to teach our youngsters concerns Christians' talents and spiritual gifts. Nearly all people, Christians and non-Christians, have various talents. Spiritual gifts are given by God to His children. They are one of many blessings given to enrich our lives as we learn to share them.

As Christian parents we need to encourage our children to develop their talents for service to God as well as for self-development. Talents used in love can be used by God to strengthen others.

God gives each Christian spiritual gifts for them to develop and use as a member of Christ's Church. We need to discover our spiritual gift(s) given us to serve God. As our children grow and after they have accepted Christ as their Lord and Savior we need to help them find, understand, and use their spiritual gifts properly.

Due to the subject, this chapter is organized differently than the preceding chapters. We will discuss talents first and then spiritual gifts.

Talents

Each of us is unique in the eyes of God. God has given each person certain talents to develop and share. With our combined talents we experience a varying degree of creativity and ability to enrich the church and enable it to work effectively for God. Some talents even inspire others to share of themselves while other talents are supportive of others' talents.

If we did not share our talents this world would be a much duller place in which to live. Talents are used to share the beauty of Christ and to further our commitment of faith.

The shy, introverted person may be a talented composer who finds it difficult to communicate verbally. A good actor or actress may find their hidden talent in needlework or woodworking projects. No matter who we are, God has provided us with a variety of talents to express our feelings and emotions. Let's explore some of the many talents a Christian person might have.

ART

Consider how the beauty of God's world can be expressed on canvas. Those who draw, paint, sketch and earnestly labor as artists make many outstanding contributions to our world. How inspired we feel as we view masterpieces such as the Last Supper. Consider the love Leonardo da Vinci felt for God. This is more than a painting, it is an expression of love and commitment to Jesus Christ. If your young person likes to draw or paint, encourage him or her to do so. Remind your child that talents are to be used to bring happiness and joy to the creator as well as the viewer.

PHOTOGRAPHY

Photography is an expression of the world around us. It takes discipline and practice to create beautiful pictures with a camera.

Almost all young people like cameras. Allow your children the use of a camera, when possible, to capture the world in their eyes. You might find, as we did, that your son or daughter will use the camera in a variety of creative ways. A camera can explore a child's world. It can help create a funny picture or an illusion of grandeur. It might even teach you something of your child's character and innermost self which was hidden from you before.

One summer our children enrolled in a photography course. It was quite an experience! Ray Jr. took a plunger and placed it on the head of the concrete frog in my birdbath. Silly, you say. Maybe, but the child expressed a sense of humor in a most unusual manner. Likewise, Mary Ann took pictures of tiny bugs which we tend to overlook as we stomp through the woods. Children often view life from different perspectives than you and I.

A child can learn of life through the eye of a camera. Who knows what it will lead to? Can you consider a more beautiful subject to photograph than clouds, a sunset, a bird soaring in the air, a tiny child or a group of friends you love? Allow your children the opportunity to explore life as they use their talents.

HANDIWORK

My memories linger for a few moments in my past. I recall sitting under a large frame, suspended from the ceiling, and watching my mother and the neighbors sew quilts. Not only were the quilts beautiful but they were needed to provide covers for our beds. Consider the countless hours of work done on a hand-stiched quilt. A lesson in patience is practiced with each stitch. And a thing of practical beauty provides warmth and comfort as we snuggle between the covers.

Still another talent in the handiwork field is needlepoint. I'm still working on a project that has a steamboat in it. My need for patience has outweighed my passion for paddlewheel steamboats. After four years I wonder if I will ever finish my project. Your child may have the creativity to work on a project such as this. Not only do many young persons enjoy projects of this sort, they also find fulfillment in their finished project.

When he has time, my husband is terrific at woodworking projects. Our hope is that one day soon he will have a workshop to tinker in and work on projects. Creating with the hands seems to be a most satisfying thing. Perhaps God has given your child the talent to build things. Maybe your son or daughter looks for pieces of wood to make things. God allows us to experience the freedom of being ourselves through our talents. As we channel our feelings by using our talents we share our personalities with others.

MUSIC

My sister-in-law, Cindy, makes me happy as I listen to her play the piano. What a beautiful gift she has for playing the piano. Her talent has been developed over a number of years as she has practiced countless hours. Cindy often uses her talent to share with others. When we speak of the ability to inspire others, music is often one of the sources of this inspiration.

God may have given your child a talent similar to Cindy's. Surely God must like the sound of beautiful music for He has allowed us to be surrounded by so much of it. Consider David, not only a king, but also a composer and a musician. How lovely is the sound of music which glorifies God.

We have, of course, only touched on the surface of music's contribution to our world. We might mention that God uses the gift of music in a special manner. Consider the beautiful sound of "The Messiah" as it fills the air. How it overjoys my heart to sing, "King of Kings, Lord of Lords, and He shall reign forever and ever." It fills my spirit to overflowing as I consider the words and hear this inspired music.

Hymns are a spiritual blessing that are shared by those who have the talent and gift of music. "It Is Well With My Soul," "Jesus, Jesus, Jesus," and a multitude of Bill Gaither's songs brighten my day when my spirits droop. Music may draw our spirits closer to our Lord as we worship Him through our expression of feelings in music. If your children enjoy music then encourage their efforts.

SCIENCE

We can scarcely comprehend the world and the contribution that science has made throughout history. Frankly, parents, our world needs more Christians who are scientists. God is the maker of the universe and of that there is no doubt. We have many young persons who have the talent and ability to serve God as scientists.

We might mention that the world of science encompasses a range of information which is limitless. Medicine comes to mind as do those who work with our environmental needs and responsibilities. Working in areas which supply us with the freedom to be ourselves is God's goal for our lives. There are varying methods of expressing our abilities, and who knows what contribution your child may make to spark a new discovery in tomorrow's world?

LITERATURE

Some of us detest reading. Many of us don't even write letters. But there is a group of people who discover this is their niche in life. Literature makes a valuable contribution to our society.

If it were within my power to erase all the smut and filth in the world as expressed in some distorted so called "adult" magazines, it would be done. What a tasteless manner in which to use a talent. Still there are many who use their talents to serve the Lord.

It is possible that your son or daughter may be a creative person and can write a short story or a novel. It doesn't take much to encourage your child to write. When words flow freely then your child finds a channel of expression. While many writers are quiet persons, their words fill page after page of books. I, myself, feel it is far easier to write my words than to speak them. You never know what talent you have until you give it the opportunity to function.

Those who write little verses of poetry find fulfillment in this talent. My late grandmother, my father's mother, Florence Mae Bascom Loftiss, composed little poems and verses. The family still enjoys reading them although she is no longer with us.

There are times when I think I'm going to give up and never

write another word. Then there are moments when I know I must write. Writing gives me the opportunity to share myself with others. Some things I write, I would seldom, if ever, share with even my best friend. Writing allows me to live a balanced life because I give of myself.

There are so many areas where each of us allows our talents to function. In our Christian community there is a need to exercise our talents more. There is a constant need for Christians to achieve great strides for our faith when we take time to share ourselves as God intended. Fears are set aside as we inspire others and receive the blessings that are ours by using our God-given talents.

Spiritual Gifts

"Every good and perfect gift is from above, coming down from the Father of the heavenly lights, who does not change like shifting shadows. He chose to give us birth through the word of truth, that we might be a kind of first fruits of all he created." James 1:17,18 (NIV)

"There are different kinds of gifts, but the same Spirit. There are different kinds of service, but the same Lord. There are different kinds of working, but the same God works all of them in all men. Now to each one the manifestation of the Spirit is given for the common good. To one there is given through the Spirit the message of wisdom, to another the message of knowledge by means of the same Spirit, to another faith by the same Spirit, to another gifts of healing by that one Spirit, to another miraculous powers, to another prophecy, to another the ability to distinguish between spirits, to another the ability to speak in different kinds of tongues, and to still another the interpretation of tongues. All these are the work of one and the same Spirit, and he gives them to each one, just as he determines." 1 Corinthians 12:4-11 (NIV)

The subject of spiritual gifts is an important one. It can also be a controversial subject. In order that this author be unbiased there will be no individual discussion on the purpose of each gift. As a fundamentalist evangelical Christian it might be unfair for

106

me to provide my personal interpertation to the area of spiritual gifts. It is a matter which can be interpreted in a variety of ways. Since my beliefs and doctrine are conservative in nature and I believe my assignment is not to discuss doctrine, I will forgo any efforts to discuss the individual spiritual gifts.

In discussing spiritual gifts it is important to realize that these gifts are to be used in serving Christ. Each new believer receives a gift or gifts from the Father. Possession of spiritual gifts serves a variety of functions throughout our Christian life. The Spirit has planned each gift knowing where we need to use them and how they will enrich our lives.

Not all Christians are using their spiritual gifts wisely or properly. In fact, many of us aren't using them at all. Spiritual gifts are building blocks for each church. There are serious voids in many churches because Christians have neglected to search out their gifts and use them for furthering the "good news" of Jesus Christ. Our gifts may vary but all are needed to balance out the body of Christ, the Church. Many of us have not allowed our gifts to function because we have been uncertain as to what our gifts may be.

A careful study of spiritual gifts may reveal hidden talents and allow you to discover what gifts you have. Not all spiritual gifts may surface at one time. It may take years to develop and mature in your faith to the point that you begin to exercise your spiritual gifts. Always bear in mind that these gifts are not for our sake or to glorify us but for the work of Christ's ministry.

A good reminder concerning our gifts: *"Each one should use whatever gift he has received to serve others, faithfully administering God's grace in its various forms."* 1 Peter 4:10 (NIV)

Once again I find myself pushed for space as I share the truths of God with you, so I must be brief. Below are listed a variety of Scripture passages which will shed new light on our topic of discussion, gifts. Please read them in your Bible and be encouraged by God's concern and desire for us to work with Him in hope that others may know Christ as you and I do.

- 1 Timothy 4:12,14
- Romans 12:11

- 1 Corinthians 3:3-7,21-23
- Ephesians 4:12

There are numerous passages on the subject. Do yourself a favor and uncover all that you can concerning this important subject. Paul has gone into great detail to describe the various gifts to us. The purpose is that we might identify them and use them properly. 1 Corinthians 12:8-10, 28-30 list a large variety of gifts, some of which we have listed above. Still others are listed in Ephesians 4:11-13 and Romans 12:3-16.

Summary

All gifts are to be used through the exercise of continual Christian love. Read 1 Corinthians 13, the "love chapter" to determine the importance of love in the Christian life. Love is, in my estimate, the most valuable of ALL gifts from God for without the love of God our efforts to serve are meaningless.

It won't be easy to discuss gifts with your young person. Perhaps it isn't supposed to be but sharing love is another matter. For you see, Christian friend, love is the key to the Christian life. Christ's love is seen over and over again throughout the Scriptures. Perfect, unselfish love, love that holds nothing of itself back from another is the most important gift of all. Teach your child the value of love as a gift to others. Allow your child to know that this gift makes the difference between a sensitive spirit and a hardened heart. Love cannot be bought or sold. But when given away it enriches the lives of others in countless ways.

So then, talents and gifts are important to our lives. The proper exercise of these ingredients brings joy, happiness, and expression of Christ's love in us together to give us a balanced Christian life. The things which God so graciously gives us are to be used not only for our enlightenment and joy but as gifts we share with others.

chapter nine

The Importance
of Prayer

Almost all Christians pray at one time or another. Some pray more often than others. The issue is not how often your children should pray but how and what they should pray. I doubt that most young persons understand the importance of prayer in their young lives. Throughout this chapter we will look at prayer through the eyes of a young person.

What Is Prayer?

To the Adult. Prayer is open communication with the living Lord. It is our opportunity, as Christians, to speak on a one-to-one basis with the One who created us. Prayer is speaking, in an open manner, to God. It is telling God what is in your heart and in your mind. It is a sincere evaluation of life. Some of the things a young person might pray about are:

- Needs for each day.
- Health.
- Overcoming temptations and struggles.
- Giving thanks for something that has been a blessing in their young life.
- Questioning God concerning something not previously understood by you.
- Intercession, that is, praying for someone else or their needs. This might include a close friend, family member, schoolmate, or any number of various needs others have.
- Praying and asking God to supply answers to some difficult questions concerning faith.
- Family problems and needs.
- Praying for forgiveness in some matter.

There are many opportunities to pray, and believe it or not, many Christian junior high students and high school students pray on a fairly regular basis.

To the Child. Prayer is the way we talk and listen to God. God wants us to talk to Him everyday about everything that bothers us. Prayer is also a time to think about God and how great He is. It is a time to praise Him and thank Him for being who He is.

Why Pray?

To the Adult. Have you ever encountered a moment when you felt so boggled down and involved in a situation that you didn't know what to do? Of course you have! So has your young person. Our children are not immune to problems and heartaches in their lives. They have bad days and good days much like you and I. Being young does not exempt a person from problems. I took a survey among a variety of young persons and it appears that many young Christians (ages 11-17) seek a time to pray on a regular basis. Their needs are varied and there are many problems which tear at their heartstrings. They want help and answers to God's will for their lives just as you and I do.

When these young persons pray, what happens? God, who already knows each need and desire of the heart, responds immediately. Although God may make us wait a while before we understand His will, His response is immediate and for our own good. Through prayer and communication with the Lord they can express their feelings and desire for guidance and help. They want to understand life and pursue happiness just like anyone else. God can truly deliver us from life's pressures and hardships at any moment. But sometimes God waits for us to discover our need for Him before results are seen. But why should your child learn to pray and how? What results will be seen as your young person uses prayer in his or her daily life? Here are some of the thoughts you and your children will find of interest on prayer. They are written to share with your youngster.

To the Child. Here are some thoughts concerning prayer:

1. God tells us to pray.
2. Prayer is an encourager and uplifter.
3. Prayer is God's way of allowing Christians to experience certain Christian joy and see results in our time spent in prayer.
4. Prayer knows no bounds and reaches all the way to where God is.
5. Prayers bring blessings.
6. Prayer is the way to gain a deeper knowledge of the Holy Spirit.
7. God teaches us from our prayer experiences.
8. Prayer makes us sensitive to God's call for us to walk closely with Him.

Prayer is a necessity in the life of the believer. Through it we find hope, inspiration, guidance, answers and assurance from the Lord. No matter how hopeless we feel in our hearts God has the answer to our need. We ourselves are limited in resolving life's problems but God can work miracles in a twinkling of the eye. Prayer is calling out to God and placing Him in authority over every situation which binds our spirits and limits our abilities to function properly. You should want prayer to be a daily part of your life.

The Importance of Prayer

To the Adult. Who among us has not cried for a solution to our dilemma? When our hearts plead for help, God hears. Our God is full of compassion and love for His children. We are His tiny infants crying out in the darkness of night. Our need is real. We need reassurance in our struggle for security. In our cry of helplessness our Father cuddles us in His loving arms and touches our lives with His wonderful love. God's concern for us is overwhelming.

God gives us prayer for many reasons. Your child should understand that prayer is an important gift from God. The more we use it the more beautiful it becomes. Even when we are unsure how to pray and what to say, words can flow from our hearts. God knows how often we do not know what words to say and although we do not communicate in words we communicate in spirit. God has promised that the Holy Spirit will even tell us what to pray. Prayers are not necessarily a series of words repeated over and over again from memory. Prayer is a heart attitude and the expressing of our innermost self to God.

Perhaps it would profit your child to realize that you (their parent, grandparent, friend, or special loved one) have prayed for their needs. What greater gift is there than the prayer of intercession for another's needs? Allow your young person to know how great your love has been for them through prayer. Prayer gives hope. Knowing that someone cares enough to pray for you shows a genuine expression of love.

Allow me to share a personal example with you. Our son, Ray, had greatly difficulty surviving the first few months of life. He was born with a respiratory problem. It was almost impossible for him to breathe. He panted using short quick breaths to supply his oxygen. I recall the doctor entering my room and saying, "I think we need to send your son to St. Vincent's Hospital in Little Rock. He has a severe problem which cannot be treated here. St. Vincent's can take proper care of him and give him the treatment he needs if he is to live."

I found it difficult to understand the words my doctor spoke. Ray was born by caesarean section and I had been given medication for the operation. My head was still a bit confused and my thoughts were fuzzy as I tried to reason through the doctor's words. All I knew was I had to pray about this matter and have others pray about it, too. We needed to send Ray to Little Rock as soon as possible.

The doctor had my bed wheeled down the hall to the baby nursery. When the curtain was opened I could scarcely stand the pain and heartache. A nurse held our baby up for me to see. I was almost in a frenzy. In my heart I knew he needed the oxygen in the incubator more than anything. I signaled for the nurse to place Ray back in the incubator so he could breathe the precious oxygen. As tears flowed from my eyes and dripped down my cheeks, I continued to pray.

Back in my room nothing seemed more important than prayer. I asked someone to call a friend in the church we attended and activate the prayer chain. Prayer was all we could offer God as this tiny child lay helpless in the hospital nursery. I recall praying and telling the Lord that this child belonged to Him and to please not let him die. This prayer was not far removed from my mind for many days as Ray lingered near death. Dozens of Christians prayed around the clock for our son's recovery and for strength for our family.

The prayers offered to God seemed to make us stronger and give us more peace with each passing day. We were allowing our faith full reign in functioning. We opened the doors of our hearts and spoke openly with our Father, God. My husband, Sandy, visited the hospital in Little Rock every day. He made the 160-mile round trip faithfully. He would stand and watch through a large glass window as the nurses tended our son. He used that driving time as a prayer time and knew God was nearer than ever before. These were trying days in our lives but God kept us strong in belief that a miracle would happen.

Late one afternoon Sandy came in from his Little Rock trip and entered my room. "Guess what, he said?"

Hoping that Ray was better I asked, "What?"

A smile found its way across his weary face and as he choked back the tears, he said, "I got to hold our son today." Needless to say our tears of happiness were plentiful. Our Lord had not only heard the prayers of many but had given us a much appreciated answer. Ray would make it. He would be home within days for us to love and care for. God had taught the importance of faith and prayer in a most difficult time in our lives. The prayers of many will never be forgotten and are cherished deeply in our hearts.

To the Child. Help your child understand that prayer is both a gift and a privilege. It is by prayer that we become personally acquainted with God. Through prayer we learn to sense His presence and start to see life through His eyes. Help your child understand that prayer is talking to their Father. Teach them to thank Him for His love and tell Him they love Him.

Jesus: Our Example for Prayer

To the Adult. Now that we have considered the importance of prayer, let's look at some Scriptures concerning prayer, the need for it, what it does, why pray, and how to pray.

"And in the early morning, while it was still dark, He arose and went out and departed to a lonely place, and was praying there. And Simon found Him, and said to Him, 'Everyone is looking for You.'" Mark 1:35,36 (NAS)

"And they came to a place named Gethsemane; and He said to His disciples, 'Sit here until I have prayed.'" Mark 14:32 (NAS)

Jesus gave us examples of prayer throughout the four gospels. Consider some of the important facts in the verses above and apply them to your personal prayer habits. (1) Jesus prayed early in the morning. (2) He went to a place to be alone. (3) Jesus sought a place of quiet and peace as He prayed. (4) Jesus was interested in not being disturbed as He prayed. (5) Jesus used no flowery phrases or expressions and stunned no one with eloquent speech as He prayed openly or privately.

Prayer is a very private matter. Although we often pray in public most private and personal prayers are spoken when we are isolated from the eyes and ears of the world. Jesus found a quiet place where He felt the presence of God in which to pray and listen to His Father. Jesus took time, and set aside a part of His day for prayer. He knew the importance of communication with the Father and did not neglect His duty and privilege to pray. Jesus, in His humanness, understood how to listen and ask for God's guidance in order that He might fully do His Father's work.

To the Child. There is no better way to express our feelings than to pray. Although God knows our hearts He still wants us to pray.

Jesus' Instruction Concerning Prayer

To the Adult. As we concentrate on Jesus' instructions concerning prayer we will use our Bible as a textbook. It is for our benefit as well as our young persons that we conduct a proper study on prayer. As we understand Jesus' words we will surely become aware of some habits Christians need to have as they pray. With these habits revealed we can lead the way to make change in wrong methods and styles of prayer. When we know how to pray and gain results in our efforts, our children will learn from our example. There is no substitute for an effective prayer life.

Matthew 6:11-18 is the Christian's guideline to prayer. Take time to read it for yourself. I believe you will agree that the Lord Jesus Christ gave a clear indication of what is proper and improper in the matter of prayer. Prayer is too important to fall into the trap of playing games with others as we pray. Jesus states with no doubt at all that there is no reward for those who make a public display of irregular and immature prayer habits. Sadly, there are those who make an exhibition of their public prayer life.

Our young persons should understand that there are men and

women who deliberately try to "put on a show" when called on to pray openly or in a church worship service. You have seen them and so have I. They pray on and on using flowery phrases that sound pleasing to our ears. Their prayers are often filled with "pet phrases" which they feel are pleasing to God. But what is it that Jesus said, "Pray like this . . ."

I think what Jesus is saying is simply this: be brief. Don't try to do a snow job on God. God knows your heart and your needs. God knows what you are trying to do and what you will say before the words ever leave your mouth. Be earnest and sincere as you pray. God is not pleased with needless "showmanship." Don't seek the approval of those around you. We are praying, not displaying, and no demonstration of eloquence is needed.

"If my people, who are called by my name, will humble themselves and pray and seek my face and turn from their wicked ways, then will I hear from heaven and will forgive their sin and will heal their land. Now my eyes will be open and my ears attentive to the prayers offered in this place. I have chosen and consecrated this temple so that my Name may be there forever. My eyes and my heart will always be there." 2 Chronicles 7:14-16 (NIV)

"Devote yourselves to prayer, keeping alert in it with an attitude of thanksgiving." Colosians 4:2 (NAS)

"Pray without ceasing; in everything give thanks; for this is God's will for you in Christ Jesus." 1 Thessalonians 5:17,18 (NAS)

"With all prayer and petition pray at all times in the Spirit, and with this in view, be on the alert with all perseverance and petition for all saints, and pray on my behalf, that utterance may be given to me in the opening of my mouth, to make known with boldness the mystery of the gospel." Ephesians 6:18,19 (NAS)

"And the prayer offered in faith will restore the one who is sick, and the Lord will raise him up, and if he has committed sins, they will be forgiven him. Therefore, confess your sins to one another, and pray for one another, so that you may be healed. The effective prayer of a righteous man can accomplish much." James 5:15,16 (NAS)

Prayer and its power should never be underestimated. When we use prayer as an effective tool to help us through difficult times then we will use it more often. It is exciting to see how God works through situations that are almost impossible. In the verses we have just read there is a wealth of information. When we let the Holy Spirit demonstrate the power prayer has in the life of the believer, then life-changing results will be seen all about us.

Through your efforts in sharing the understanding you have gained of prayer, your young person should respond to a desire to learn more about how to pray. What then will you tell them?

1. Prayer is private communication with our loving Father.
2. Prayer is an opportunity to see and experience God at work in your daily life.
3. Prayer is speaking our needs to our Father who already knows our hearts.
4. Prayer is being honest and open about life.
5. Prayer is a true expression of needs and concerns.
6. Prayer is asking God to be a vital part of our lives.
7. Prayer is our way of telling God we know He is our strength.
8. Prayer is an exercise of faith.
9. Prayer allows us to believe and expect God to give answers, supply needs and work through us to make our faith stronger and more mature.
10. Prayer is setting worries and heartaches aside and allowing God to handle life's painful situations.
11. Prayer is asking God for relief, guidance or help for ourselves or for another.
12. Prayer allows us to listen for God to speak to our hearts.
13. Prayer is knowing that our God is not far away or distant but is a part of our being. Recall the Holy Spirit lives within us and is an important part of our spiritual lives.

14. Prayer goes on and on, never ceasing. Prayer is never out of date or completely finished. Prayer is our open channel to God.

15. Prayer gives praise, thanks, makes petitions, asks forgiveness, makes intercessions and opens the door of our spirit to receive the blessings of God.

To the Child. I want to teach you more about prayer. Let's think about what prayer is and how we can use it. (Use this chapter as a guide.)

Who Prays?

To the Adult. If your child asked you such a pointed question, how would you respond? It is difficult to imagine that there are people who never pray, isn't it? But the sad fact is that few people exercise the right to pray.

All of us should pray on a regular basis. Personally, I find it difficult to get the day started without some prayer time. Every day seems to have something special about it. There is always someone or something to pray about. Were it not for the blessing of prayer and our belief in Christ, life would be difficult to endure. The world seems hopelessly lost and drowning in a sea of turmoil. But regardless of how often you and I pray there are millions of Christians who seldom, if ever, pray at all.

The person who prays is a person who is thankful, gives praise, has needs or requests and/or is seeking to draw closer to the Lord. Everyone can pray. The tiny child can utter a simple prayer and have the assurance that God has heard. Kings, presidents, senators, congressmen, ministers, teachers, blue collar workers, white collar workers, old people, young ones; prayer knows no limits. It is only limited by the individual who is unwilling to use it effectively.

To the Child. All of us should pray, everyday, in a special quiet time. When we wait for God's answers to prayer we will find them. Prayer should be used at all stages of your life to help you grow through the good times and the bad.

How Can Prayer Affect Your Life?

To the Adult. Do the sunshine and rain affect your life in the slightest? Of course they do. So it is with prayer. Your young person can realize, with some guidance on your part, that prayer can make a vast difference in life's situations. Prayer opens the door for all kinds of opportunities and adventures.

God works miracles in a twinkling of the eye. Nothing is impossible for God. As we pray God acts. Although there are moments when we wait for answers to prayer and wonder if God has forgotten us, we can be assured that God has our best interest in mind. With the answering of prayers there is a certain feeling of reassurance. God changes lives through prayer. We grow in faith through exercising a regular prayer habit. We should never underestimate the wonder and power of prayer in our lives. It is a "power pill" for our weary souls.

Prayer can bring about needed changes in life. God's will is that prayer be used to pour out our hearts so that we can openly become aware of our continual need for God's special love. When the frustrations of the world cause us to fold up and hide our emotions prayer will help us re-establish contact with the Father. God teaches us that things aren't as hopeless as we thought when we see prayers answered.

Important Information

Some important thoughts concerning prayer are:

- Pray to the Father. Matthew 6:9.
- Begin prayer with thanking God (Adoration). Psalms 75:1, Psalms 34:3, Psalms 116:12, Philippians 4:6.

- Praise God for the things He has done in your life and the lives of others. Psalms 34:1-3, Colossians 1:15-20, Philippians 2:9-11, 2 Timothy 6:15 are all fine examples of prayers of praise.
- Confess any sins in your life that you might experience full fellowship with God. 1 John 1:9, John 8:34,36, Romans 5:1.
- Pray for others (Intercession). James 5:14-20, 2 Chronicles 7:14, Romans 1:9, Psalms 28:9, 1 Timothy 2:1.
- Make your requests known to God in honesty and simplicity (Petition). Hebrews 4:15,16, John 16:24, Luke 11:13, James 4:2 are Scriptures which should help you understand this idea in depth.
- Know that God has answered your prayer in the manner best suited for your life.
- Listen for the instruction. Be still and experience the presence of God. Psalms 46:10, Hebrews 3:15.

There are many blessings in understanding what prayer does. Help your children seek out God. Allow them to understand God has placed your prayer request at the top of His Master list and answers it personally.

Below is a brief list of verses which should encourage and lift your spirits on the subject of prayer. Read them to gain more insight on the subject of prayer:

- Ephesians 6:11-18
- Luke 18:1
- Mark 11:22-24
- Hebrews 3:1
- 1 John 1:3
- 1 John 3:22
- Hebrews 7:25
- Colossians 1:2
- Psalms 66:18
- John 15:7
- 1 John 5:14,15
- 1 Thessalonians 5:17
- 1 Timothy 2:1-8
- Romans 8:26,27
- Ephesians 1:17-19

Never be afraid to ask God anything. Prayer is given to us in order that we might verbalize our thoughts to God. There is nothing we can approach Him about that is news to Him. When you or your young person know that your request is heard, evaluated, and then acted upon by God then you can be sure God's ultimate will shall be done.

Here are some passages concerning our need to ask for the things we need.

"But if any of you lacks wisdom, let him ask of God, who gives to all men generously and without reproach, and it will be given to him. But let him ask in faith without any doubting, for the one who doubts is like the surf of the sea driven and tossed by the wind." James 1:5,6 (NAS)

"If you remain in union with me and my words remain in you, you may ask whatever you please and you shall have it." John 15:7 (Williams)

"And anything you ask for as bearers of my name I will do for you, so that the Father may be glorified through the Son. Yes, I repeat it, anything you ask for as bearers of my name I will do it for you." John 14:13,14 (Williams)

When you do not believe that your request will be answered by God more than likely it will not. But if in your heart you feel that your request will ultimately honor and glorify God and God, in fact, agrees then your request will be honored.

There are many instances when we do not receive from God because we never dare to ask. We miss special opportunities because we do not ask God with a sincere heart. We think our need isn't important and we don't want to bother God. You see, our lack of nerve or our fear of rejection often keeps us from claiming the gifts God holds in store for us. We often fear the unknown, don't we? But we should remember that our Father,

God, wants us to have His best and whatever He has stored away for us is ours for the asking. Everything that concerns us is of deep importance to God. There are no unimportant prayers.

You might teach your children to ask these questions of themselves before they ask anything of God.

1. Is this thing good for me?
2. Is it really an important need in my life or the life of another?
3. How will God view my request?
4. Is there anything selfish and ungodly in my request?
5. Am I ready for whatever answer God gives me?
6. Am I willing to wait a little longer for an answer?
7. How will getting this thing change my life?
8. How will this affect others?
9. Will this strengthen my relationship with Christ?
10. Can God receive open praise for answering this prayer?
11. Will this make my commitment to Christ stronger?
12. Do I really believe this prayer request is pleasing to God?

To the Child. If your children can consider some of these points as they ask in prayer for God's blessings, then their decisions will be much wiser. Prayer is important and should not be misused. We do not use it to "get the things we want" but to supply our daily needs. With that thought in mind let us press on knowing that proper prayer is pleasing to God. The key to proper prayer is an unselfish and giving attitude.

In setting guidelines for your child's prayer time be sure to reassure him or her that all prayers are heard by God. All prayers are important but sometimes we have to wait for God to answer.

Encourage your youngster in praying. Help them discover an effective manner in which to pray. Pray openly with your child. Allow them to see your faith in action as you get on your knees and pray.

chapter ten

Growing in Faith and in Love

Introduction

Throughout our study we have come to understand that faith is the key to a personal relationship with God. Faith combined with true understanding of Christlike love will provide for a well balanced Christian life. In this chapter we will strive to share some important facts concerning faith and love with our children.

Faith and love are taught to our children by example more than by explanation. We will depart once more from our usual format because of the subject matter. Study the material presented in this chapter, apply it to your life, and then share the Scriptures and thoughts with your children.

Faith

It is necessary to have faith to trust and believe the words of the Scriptures. We cannot expect our children to gain this faith and allow it to function without our having some involvement in their lives. We, as parents, family, friends and caring individuals, must share our faith with a sincere heart and allow our children to choose for themselves the course they will take. It is, of course, our greatest hope that their decisions will lead them into a personal relationship with Jesus Christ as Lord, Savior, and Redeemer of their lives.

Faith comes by hearing the Word of God and love is faith in action. Allow faith to take root within your spirit and care for it tenderly and gently as it grows. The Christian life is a combination of sunshine and rain. None of us is immune from hurt and problems and yet all of us are exposed to the beautiful light of Christ as we learn about God and His might and majesty as displayed in the Scriptures. But how is this faith developed?

First and perhaps most important of all is to buy your children a readable version of the Bible. There is plenty of time, a lifetime in fact, for them to grow into the ever-popular King James version of the Bible. As a Sunday School teacher and a worker with children allow me to impress you with some of the feelings and attitudes children have as they struggle to understand the word of God.

1. *Confusion.* Children are confused by the King James version. This confusion can discourage a young person so that he or she never desires to read even the first verse of Scripture.

2. *Frustration.* Children can and often do become so frustrated as they read the Bible that they become "spiritual dropouts." They want to understand and yet they can't. Oftentimes children will not share this with a parent because their parents, after choosing a Bible for them, made quite an ordeal over sharing their gift. Children don't want to embarrass their parents and often say nothing about their frustrations as they struggle to understand the Bible.

3. *Rebellion.* A young person might rebel because the Bible isn't easy to understand. "I don't know what that means," is often heard by the Sunday School teacher who has gained the confi-

dence of the class. This rebellion is due to the fact that a difficult-to-understand translation makes children feel inferior or "dumb." There are no "dumb" students, only those who do not truly understand.

These are a few of the events which can turn a young person away from the desire to learn the Word of God. It is difficult to become involved in something which is completely foreign to you. My suggestion is that you might consider buying an easier to read version such as a beginner Bible. Recall when you first started to read, the teacher didn't hand you a copy of Shakespeare and ask you to read aloud and interpret its meaning for the class. If the teacher had done such a thing it is doubtful many of us would have learned to read at all. Instead, you and I learned to read a few simple words at a time. "See Spot. Run Spot, run. See Jane. Run Jane. Run Jane, run."

Do you see now what the average child has to deal with when he or she tries to read a complex version of the Scriptures? Frustrations, fear, rebellion, and feelings of low self-esteem often overcome what spiritual feelings a child has simply because the words written on the page cannot be comprehended. Children can, in fact, turn their back on God because of this problem in their lives.

What translation should you use with your child? There are many good ones available and I would like to suggest two of them.

1. The New International Version
2. The Living Bible

Also, I find the Williams New Testament, the Phillips New Testament, and the Good News Bible good as alternate versions. The need is to understand the Word of God, apply it to your heart and then to use it in your daily life. Isn't that true? Well, to make these things happen we must first understand what we are reading. There is time to move up to a deeper translation such as the King James, New King James, or the New American Standard at a later date. Your children will let you know when they are ready to learn more and then you can change to another version, and they are on their way.

Love

A life without the love of God in it is meaningless. It searches for a meaning to life and a reason to live. To love others, as God intends us to love, we must first love God. God is the Supreme source of love.

Love is expressed in various ways: a mother's tears, a loving bear hug, a little kiss, or a wink of the eye that indicates concern. Love is an ongoing process. Real love stays intact and does not run away at the first sign of trouble.

The Scriptures have placed great emphasis on the value of love. Let's look at an assortment of Scriptures in order that you might decide what to tell your children concerning love. This study will be detailed so you may want to use your Bible as a reference and make notes.

"I give you a new command, to love one another. Just as I have loved you, you too must love one another. By this everybody will know that you are my disciples, if you keep on showing love for one another." John 13:34-35 (Williams)

Question: How did Jesus love his disciples? *Answer:* He gave them considerable attention, taught them on a one-to-one basis as well as in a group. He prayed for them. He shared hardships and good times with them. He listened to them, showed them the truths of God, and cared for them very deeply. The love Jesus displayed was God's love, unselfish and it concentrated on the individual's needs. The love Christ displayed was an example of Godly love bestowed on mankind.

Jesus also demonstrated that our love is to be of the same quality and intensity toward one another.

Read 1 John 4:7-16 (Williams). Verses 7 and 8 read, *"Dearly beloved, let us practice loving one another, because love originates with God, and everyone who practices loving is a child of God and knows God by experience. Whoever does not love has never come to know God by experience, because God is love."*

To us, the greatest demonstration of God's love for us was sending His only Son into the world to give us life through Him. We see real love, not in the fact that we loved God, but that He loved us and sent His Son to make a personal atonement for our sins. If God loved us as much as that, surely we, in our turn, should love each other!

It is true that no human being has ever had a direct vision of God. Yet if we love each other God does actually live within us, and His love grows in us towards perfection. And the guarantee of our living in Him and His living in us is the share of His own Spirit which He gives us.

We ourselves are eyewitnesses, able and willing to testify to the fact that the Father did send the Son to save the world. Everyone who acknowledges that Jesus is the Son of God finds that God lives in him, and he lives in God. So have we come to know and trust the love God has for us. God is love, and the man whose life is lived in love does, in fact, live in God, and God does, in fact, live in him.

Once again we have found Scriptures which overwhelm our Christian spirit. For within these verses are the very basics of the Christian life. These passages are, in fact, the very heart of the message of salvation through Jesus Christ. Let us look at them individually and allow the Holy Spirit to speak to our hearts.

"Let us go on loving one another:" This phrase teaches me that love has manifested itself within the hearts of these people. Love has been established among them and John says, "Let us go on loving."

In fact this phrase tells me not to turn my back on or refuse to love another Christian but to keep on. Share the love you have in your heart. Your young person should be taught that God's love is a sign of strength not a signal of weakness. There is no shame or fear in the perfect love God gives.

"Love comes from God:" God is the ultimate source of love. It is not self-centered or selfish but concerned for others.

"The man who does not love cannot know Him at all, for

God is love:" Doesn't this phrase explain itself? Yes, it does! The person who does not love cannot know God at all for God is love. Plant the seed of love firmly within the life of your child and watch how God will develop it into something lovely.

"The greatest demonstration of God's love for us has been His sending His only Son into the world to give us life through Him. We see real love, not in the fact that we love God, but that he loved us and sent his Son to make personal atonement for our sins." Within the space of two sentences the writer of 1 John has told us God's plan for mankind.

You see, many Christians really don't understand how deeply God does love us. Either they have not realized it or not allowed this truth to become personal to them. Until a person realizes that Jesus Christ really died for them, personally, then it is impossible to experience the full love of God flowing in his or her life. Ask your children to close their eyes as you read this verse to them. Ask them if they see Jesus in their mind. Do you see Jesus teaching, healing, caring for all those who need Him? Do you see the soldiers dragging Jesus away? What's happening now? Now Jesus has been turned over to the people and is being placed on a cross. The nails are being driven into His hands and feet.

Jesus is hanging on the cross and is in great pain. He knows that He must die for our sins. He wants to clear the record and set it straight so that you and I might experience eternal life. Jesus looks down from the cross and sees you. He speaks your name (child's name), saying, *"I love you. I came to set you free so that you might have everlasting life and live with my Father and Me forever and forever."*

What do you feel as Jesus speaks to you? Do you understand what Jesus has done? Do you want to accept Jesus' gift of salvation (eternal life)? If God loves us as much as that, surely we, in turn should love each other!

This is not a tactic using sympathy to have your children come to Christ. It is God speaking to your children and wanting them to understand the gift He has to offer, eternal life.

"If we love each other God does actually live within us, and His love grows in us towards perfection." We know, of course,

from our previous studies that the Holy Spirit lives within the believer. It is this Spirit that God gives us as our guide and protector.

"The guarantee of our living in Him and His living in us is the share of His own Spirit which He gives." We have a guarantee from God that a share of His Spirit lives within us. There should be no problem with sharing the idea of what a guarantee is and does. In fact your child should be told that God's guarantee of eternal life never runs out.

"The Father did send the Son to save the world. Everyone who acknowledges that Jesus is the Son of God finds that God lives in him, and he lives in God." Here is a passage I searched for when I began to grow as a Christian. This is a passage of reassurance and comfort. It is true! God does not lie. God acknowledges us as His own because we have accepted Jesus' gift of salvation. What a blessing that should give to our hearts. We need never forget how great the love of the Father is for us.

"So have we come to know and trust the love God has for us." God has not left us to wander through life without purpose. God has many things to share with us as we commit our lives to Him. Show your child the words "know" and "trust." Recall how we have talked about believing as knowing and trusting God for all things.

"God is love, and the man whose life is lived in love does, in fact, live in God, and God does, in fact, live in him." What joy and pleasure that should give anyone who will believe and trust God through Jesus Christ, our Lord and Savior.

"Dear children, let us stop loving with words or lips alone, but let us love with actions and in truth." 1 John 3:18 (Williams) Love is put into action and practice in our lives. It does not dry up from lack of use or fade away throughout the years. Discuss with your child that love is not a mind thought, kept and stored away only to think of from time to time. Love is doing and being God's person all the time.

"Just as the Father has loved Me, I have also loved you; abide in My love. If you keep My commandments, you will abide in My

love; just as I have kept My Father's commandments, and abide in His love."

"These things I have spoken to you, that My joy may be in you, and that your joy may be made full. This is My commandment, that you love one another, just as I have loved you. Greater love has no one than this, that one lay down his life for his friends." John 15:9-13 (NAS)

"And now I will show you the most excellent way. If I speak in the tongues of men and of angels, but have not love, I am only a resounding gong or a clanging cymbal. If I have the gift of prophecy and can fathom all mysteries and all knowledge, and if I have a faith that can move mountains, but have not love, I am nothing. If I give all I possess to the poor and surrender my body to the flames, but have not love, I gain nothing. Love is patient, love is kind. It does not envy, it does not boast, it is not proud. It is not rude, it is not self-seeking, it is not easily angered, it keeps no record of wrongs. Love does not delight in evil but rejoices with the truth. It always protects, always trusts, always hopes, always perserveres. Love never fails." 1 Corinthians 12:31b, 13:1-8a (NIV)

This verse gives a clear demonstration concerning the power of love in the life of the Christian. Were we not to exercise the privilege of loving, as Christ commanded us, then we would rob ourselves of some of life's greatest joys. Love is involved and caring. Loving is giving and not expecting a reward in return.

Faith and love walk hand in hand together. Each is important in building our Christian character. Throughout each chapter we have learned a great deal about God. God is the ultimate love in the life of the Christian. It is important to speak of God's love as never failing and being consistent as we discuss God with our children.

"For the Father Himself loves you, because you have loved Me, and have believed that I came forth from the Father." John 16:27 (NAS) Only as your child learns to love Christ can love from God be learned.

"For this reason, I bow my knees before the Father, from whom every family in heaven and on earth derives its name, that He would grant you, according to the riches of His glory, to be strengthened with power through His Spirit in the inner man; so that Christ may dwell in your hearts through faith; and that you, being rooted and grounded in love, may be able to comprehend with all the saints what is the breadth and length and heights and depth, and to know the love of Christ which surpasses all knowledge, that you may be filled up to all the fullness of God." Ephesians 3:14-19 (NAS)

Lastly, in sharing our thoughts concerning love comes a statement of fact from the apostle Paul. It in fact states my feeling as well as his certainty as to our position in Christ. Discuss it with your children and allow them to search out God with your loving guidance.

"Who shall separate us from the love of Christ? Shall tribulation, or distress, or persecution, or famine, or nakedness, or peril, or sword?

Just as it is written, For Thy sake we are being put to death all day long; we were considered as sheep to be slaughtered, but in all these things we overwhelmingly conquer through Him who loved us.

> *For I am convinced that neither*
> *death,*
> *nor life,*
> *nor angels,*
> *nor principalities,*
> *nor things present,*
> *nor things to come,*
> *nor powers,*
> *nor height,*
> *nor depth,*
> *nor any other created thing,*
> *shall be able to separate us from the love of God, which*
>   *is in*
> *Christ Jesus our Lord."* Romans 8:35-39 (NAS)

This chapter is a different one which focused on important subject matter. In talking about faith you might say, faith is simply believing that what God says is true. Faith in God is trusting God's love to work in your life.

To the Child. It is good to have faith in God because God loves us. The love of God is greater than anything you can think of or will ever see. Love is the key to life that brings gladness and happiness. Share your faith and love with someone new each day.

chapter eleven

Questions of Interest to Children

This last chapter deals with a variety of questions. The curious mind of a child is often filled with questions which cause parents to wonder how to answer. Perhaps the questions your child will ask will be among those we answer here. So here are some ideas for your own personal consideration.

1. *Why can't we see God?* Remember we talked about God being a Spirit. If God wanted to He could make Himself visible at any time. Perhaps if we were to see God we wouldn't know how to react to Him. Some of us might be afraid of Him, some might try to follow Him everywhere He went, some might even run from Him because they have not done the things God told them to.

God is very wise and knows what is best for us. The Bible tells us that we, as Christians, will spend eternity with God. I expect then God will reveal Himself to us in all His glory and majesty.

2. *Why is it so hard to obey God's commands?* Our human nature, the one we are born with, is set on having its own way. Most of us want to have all the things we set our minds on. That is not good! Some of us fall into the trap of wanting more and more and never think about God.

It is only as we begin to let God work in our lives and become aware of Jesus' gift of eternal life (salvation) that our old human nature can change. When we become Christians we take on a new spirit (new birth). We begin to change our old habits because we want to be like Jesus.

The main reason we find it hard to obey God's commandments is because we are somewhat selfish and want our own way. This is not God's way. God wants us to be loving and giving to others. Through this we will begin to follow God's commandments a little better. It doesn't happen all at once. It takes time and a real desire to follow God's commands but you can do it.

3. *What does it mean to be a Christian?* Being a Christian means many things. It means:

- Accepting Jesus Christ as Lord and Savior.
- Believing that Jesus really did die for your sins.
- Wanting to have a better life and be different than you are now.
- Learning to follow Jesus Christ's examples of living.
- Caring more for others than you do for yourself.
- Learning to love with a different point of view.
- Sharing your life with others.
- Learning to pray and listen for the Holy Spirit to speak to your spirit.
- Turning away from the bad and sinful things in your life and starting a better and a new way of life.
- Asking forgiveness and telling God you want to repent (change your ways).
- Learning more about Jesus and God through reading your Bible and having fellowship with other Christians.

4. *Why do we need to go to go to Sunday school and church?* When we attend Sunday School and church many wonderful things can happen. First of all we can learn more about Jesus.

Secondly, there are many Christian people there. They love Jesus and have a different view on life than the person who does not believe in Jesus. Thirdly, you can discover how much you have in common with other Christians when you share your life with them. Fourth, there is a special Spirit, the Spirit of Jesus Christ, present when Christians gather together. This Spirit brings comfort, love, happiness and unites our spirits with the spirit of other Christians.

5. *Sometimes I feel like God doesn't love me. Is it possible that God does not love me anymore?* Even when we feel unloved we can know that God does love us. God's ultimate desire is for us to realize his complete and total love for you and me. Even when God must punish us, it is done in love. God has not turned His back on you and I. In fact, His love is so deep for us that He sent His only Son to earth to die for our sins.

God is always concerned for us. Although we don't always feel loved the truth is that God's love for us is limitless. If God did not love us, He would have never provided a way for us to become members of the family of God. To sacrifice His son as an atonement for sin is a total act of love.

When you really don't feel the love of God in your heart turn to the book of 1 John in the New Testament and begin to read. The words there give joy and comfort to even the youngest of heart. Then reread John 3:16 and Romans 8.

6. *How can I believe the Bible is true? "All Scripture is inspired by God and profitable for teaching, for reproof, for correction, for training in righteousness; that the man of God may be adequate, equipped for every good work."* 2 Timothy 3:16,17 (NAS)

God has left nothing out in our needs for spiritual growth. The Bible is our textbook for life and it reveals God to us. Throughout the teachings of the Bible, God reveals Himself to us and points the way to eternal life through Jesus Christ.

7. *Can I do something so bad in my life that God will not forgive me?* As a Christian we cannot expect to be perfect. God knows our hearts and knows each of us has weaknesses. While lying,

cheating, stealing, killing, harming others, adultery, and many other things cause sin in our lives, we can seek forgiveness and receive it immediately. God does not hold sin over our head and weigh us down with our wrongdoings. When we confess our sins God is just and ready to forgive us. We are forgiven immediately and God forgets about that sin because Jesus has already accepted the punishment for our sin.

There is only one sin that I know of that God does not forgive: *"Blasphemy against the Spirit shall not be forgiven."* (Matthew 12:31b) This is open rejection of the Spirit of God. It can be committed by unbelievers as well as believers. This sin grieves the Holy Spirit and quenches the efforts of the Holy Spirit to touch the life of the sinner. The Holy Spirit can be sinned against because the Spirit is God.

8. *How does God speak to us today?* Recall that we had a detailed study on the purpose of the Holy Spirit. If you still struggle with how God speaks to you reread this section of our study. The Holy Spirit, within the life of the Christian, is our teacher, helper, and guide. He was sent to us by Jesus to teach us the things of God.

9. *How can my life be of any value to God? "Are not two sparrows sold for a cent? And yet not one of them will fall to the ground apart from your Father. But the very hairs of your head are all numbered. Therefore do not fear, you are of more value than many sparrows."* Matthew 10:29-31 (NAS)

This Scripture tells us that nothing is unimportant to God. Even a tiny sparrow is known by God. Nothing happens of which God is unaware. You are very precious to God and God wants you to understand that. He has a purpose for you being on this earth. God wants you to share your life with Him so that others might come to know Him through your life.

10. *Why are the words we speak important? "And I say to you, that every careless word that men shall speak, they shall render account for it in the day of judgment. For by your words you shall be justified, and by your words you shall be condemned."* Matthew 12:36,37 (NAS)

Careless words not only hurt others but they break down the spirit of the person to whom wrong was spoken. Have you ever had anyone say unkind or thoughtless words to you? More than likely you have. It hurts our feelings when someone is deliberately unkind to us.

The Bible teaches that it is wrong to speak careless words and rattle on recklessly. We will have to account for our careless acts and deeds on the Day of Judgment. Let your words be seasoned with kindness and love so others might realize that you belong to Jesus Christ.

11. *Will going to Sunday school and church get me to heaven?* As good as it is to go to Sunday School and church, these alone will not get you to heaven. The only way to get to heaven is by believing in Jesus Christ as Savior. Jesus washed away our sins and wrong attitudes. When we take Jesus' gift, believe it, and allow that truth to be real to us, then we have assurance of eternal life.

12. *Where is Jesus now?* Jesus is in heaven with His Father. He is sitting at the right hand of God. When you hear this phrase understand that it means that Jesus is sitting very near God. He is not in some far removed place but within touching distance of God. To know this and consider how close the relationship is between God and Jesus should make you very happy. You see, Jesus is very close to us too because He loves us. Mark 16:19

13. *Why do people make fun of Christians?* Because there is great disbelief in their hearts. They do not understand the blessing that comes through knowing Jesus as Lord and Savior. They poke fun at the unknown to cover up their feelings. It is easy to make fun of something you do not understand or know nothing about. The Bible says that when Jesus comes again He will reprove these unbelievers. John 16:8

14. *What can I do when I am tempted?* 1 Corinthians 10:13 teaches us that with any temptation that comes our way there is a way of escape. God has a way out for you so that your temptation will not lead you astray. But you must want to get away from temptation or else you won't. God doesn't want temptation to

lead you into sin and so He has a way out. Your job is to look for it and call upon the name of Jesus. Resist the devil and he will flee from you.

15. *When prayers are unanswered what is the reason?* God answers our prayers the moment we speak them. There are times when God makes us wait before the answer is clear but sometimes we must wait. The Father loves us and wants what is best for us. When we pray He will answer in the manner that is best for us.

Some Scriptures about prayer are:

- John 15:16,17
- James 4:8-10
- Ephesians 2:18
- Psalms 34:4-6
- Psalms 81:7
- 2 Corinthians 12:8
- Psalms 138:3
- Psalms 34:15-17
- Zechariah 13:9
- Hebrews 4:16

16. *Does the devil have horns, a long tail and a pitchfork like my friends say he does?* No, he does not! The Scriptures teach us something quite different than you might expect about Satan. Some facts about him are:

- He was created wise.
- He was created beautiful.
- He fell into sin because he desired to be God.
- He is the prince of this world.
- He is a liar.
- He works in an effort to lead us into disobedience.
- He is wicked.
- He is clever.
- He will finally be destroyed in the last days.

Some verses you might want to read concening Satan and his character are:

- Ezekiel 28:15
- Ezekiel 28:16-19
- Matthew 12:29
- Isaiah 14:15-17
- John 8:44
- 2 Corinthians 4:4
- Matthew 13:19,38
- Ephesians 2:2
- Matthew 4:3

17. *Does God really adopt us when we become Christians?* John 1:12, Ephesians 2:19, 1 John 3:1-10, and Romans 8:14-29 all speak about our adoption into the Family of God. When we are adopted by God we belong to His Family forever. We aren't thrown out of the family because we can't live up to His standards. In fact, as members of the family, we learn together and grow in knowledge of God. What a beautiful, priceless gift, to be adopted into the Family of God.

18. *Will Jesus ever come back to earth?* Yes, He will. Here are some verses which teach this idea in depth:

- Job 19:25
- Matthew 16:27,28
- Matthew 24:3-44
- Matthew 26:64
- Mark 14:62
- Luke 12:37-40
- Luke 21:27-36
- John 14:3
- Colossians 4:5
- 1 Thessalonians 4:15-17

Allow no one to deceive you, friend, Jesus Christ will return. When He returns to earth He will take those who belong to Him back to heaven with Him. There will be happiness and rejoicing on our part for the King of Kings has taken us to live with Him throughout eternity. No more skinned knees, broken bones, tears, sickness, death or problems when we go to heaven with Jesus.

19. *How long is eternity?* Eternity cannot be measured in human terms. Eternity goes on and on and on. Our time with God will never end as we belong to the Family of God. Christians have a great deal to look forward to. We cannot imagine how long eternity will go on but our hearts should be glad to know with whom we will spend it.

God has provided for us in a special manner. As we spend eternity with Him we are secure and unshakable. Those with us are fellow believers in Jesus Christ. We have a great life to live as we accept Jesus as Savior. We are confident in knowing that Christ's gift of salvation has set us free and we will reside forever in the House of the Lord.

Appendix

THE GROWTH OF LOVE

Age level	Focal point of love	Aspect of love needed
Infant	Parents, especially the mother	To be held in parent's arms, to be nursed
Preschool child	Parents, some close friends	To be secure in the family circle
Elementary school child	Parents, school friends, neighbor friends	To be a part of home, school, and friends
Junior high young person	Friends, parents, other sex	To be accepted by friends, parents, and other sex
High school young person	Friends, other sex, parents	To date, but also to be part of original family
Young adult	Other sex, friends, parents	To marry and/or to enjoy secure relationships with friends
Parents	Children, mate, friends	To enjoy a secure marriage and to give oneself in love to children

THE GROWTH OF LOVE (continued)

Age level	Focal point of love	Aspect of love needed
Older adults	Mate, children and grand-children, friends	To have a mature marriage, acceptance by children and grandchildren, and friends

From *Childhood Education in the Church*, edited by Roy B. Zuck and Robert E. Clark. © 1975 Moody Press, Moody Bible Institute of Chicago. Used by permission.

It is important that you, the parent or teacher, recognize not only the learning level of your child, but also the need level. When you do, you will be able to bring God's truth to work on specific needs in that child's life. We must not be satisifed to teach subject matter without reference to daily living, and that includes daily personal needs.

WHAT A CHILD OF TWO AND THREE CAN LEARN

About God	God loves him.
	God takes care of him.
	God loves and cares for his family.
	God provides sun and rain.
	God does good for people.
	God is all about him.
	God wants him to talk with Him.
	God made the world.
	God made him.
	He can praise God by singing and praying.
	He can tell God he is sorry for the bad things he does.
	He should please and obey God.
About Jesus	Jesus loves him.
	Jesus once lived on earth, but now is in heaven.
	Jesus is God's Son.
	Jesus is a Friend.
	Jesus said good things which are in the Bible.
	Jesus was once a child like him.

About the Bible	The Bible tells about God. The Bible is a good Book. The Bible is a special Book. He should love the Bible.
About home and parents	God gave parents. He should obey parents.
About church and Sunday school	Church is a place to learn about God. Church is a place to see friends. Church is God's house. He should like to go to church. He can give money to God's house to help buy things.
About others	God gives grownups to care for him. Others may be good friends. Others may sometimes be unkind. Jesus wants him to be kind to others and share with them.
About angels and last things	Angels came to tell people when Jesus was born. Angels love God and praise Him.

WHAT A CHILD OF FOUR AND FIVE CAN LEARN

About God	God loves him and others. God cares for all who love Him. God cares for and loves families. God made all things. God is to be trusted and depended on. God is everywhere. God will hear prayer any time. God sent Jesus to die for sin. God wants him to be thankful for all He has made. God wants him to obey Him by obeying his parents. God loves him.
About Jesus	Jesus loves him and is his best friend. Jesus came to be the Saviour. Jesus is now living in heaven. Jesus will help him obey and share.

	Jesus wants all children to love Him.
	Jesus is always with him.
	Jesus died for him.
	Jesus can help him do hard things.
About the Bible	The Bible tells about God.
	The Bible is God's Word.
	God tells us what He wants us to do in the Bible.
	The Bible helps him know what to do.
	The Bible is a Book of true stories.
About home and parents	God gave parents to care for him and teach him.
	God gave parents to pray for him.
	He should obey his parents.
	He should want to love and please his parents.
	He sins when he disobeys his parents or is unkind.
About church and Sunday school	Church is a place to learn, sing, and worship God.
	Church is a place to meet with others who love the Lord.
	Church is a special place.
	Church is a place where we learn about God.
About others	God made all people.
	God loves everyone and wants all to love Him.
	God wants him to tell others of Jesus.
	Others may not share as he does.
	Others may be loving and kind to him.
	He is to be kind, share, and pray for others.
	God wants him to share his money.
	God wants people to help others.
About angels and last things	Some angels are good and some are bad.
	Satan (the devil) is a bad angel who did not want to please God.
	Satan and his angels want us to do bad things.

WHAT A CHILD OF SIX AND SEVEN CAN LEARN

About God	God loves him and his family and his friends.
	God loves all the people of the world.
	God wants people to love Him too.

God wants people to give their lives to Him.
God provides food for men by letting plants grow.
God takes care of the world He made.
God is good, but He is also against evil.
God wants us to pray and read our Bibles.
God is holy and cannot fail.
God has all power to help him.

About Jesus	Jesus is the Son of God.
	Jesus came to earth to die for sin.
	Jesus wants people to accept Him as their personal Saviour.
	Jesus wants to help people go to God.
	Jesus wants to take sin from our lives.
	Jesus never did anything wrong.
	Jesus rose from the dead and lives in heaven.
	Jesus loves us and wants to be our friend.
	Jesus did many wonderful miracles while on earth.
	Jesus can help him choose to do the right things.
About the Bible	The Bible is God's Book, for it tells about Him.
	The Bible tells us what God wants.
	The Bible tells how God worked with others.
	The Bible tells much about us.
	The Bible is a good Book to study, for it helps us.
	The Bible should be read and memorized.
	The Bible contains sixty-six books.
	The Bible has two major parts, called the Old and New Testaments.
About home and parents	Parents are God's leaders for us on earth.
	Parents want to help us, so we should obey them.
	Parents love us, so we should love them too.
	Parents provide food and clothing and home for us.
	God is an important guest in our home at all times.
About church and Sunday School	Church is God's house.
	Church is a place where God's people go.
	Church is a happy place.
	Church is a place for songs and prayer and Bible study.
	Church needs our help to keep it clean and quiet.

	Church is not just a building but also the people in it.
	He can give to the Lord's work through the church.
About others	Others may want the same thing he does; he must share.
	Others may not want to do the same thing he does; he must learn to give in halfway.
	Others may need something very much; he must learn to give.
	Others may be in trouble; he must learn to pray.
	Others may be unkind; he must learn to forgive.
	Others may not know Jesus; he must learn to tell them about him.
About angels and last things	Satan tempts us to sin and disobey God.
	Good angels worship and praise God.
	Good angels are God's servants.
	Jesus has gone to heaven to prepare a place there for all who love Him.
	Jesus is coming to take us to live with Him forever.

WHAT A CHILD OF EIGHT AND NINE CAN LEARN

About God	God is all powerful, all wise, and everywhere.
	God is present with him at all times.
	God wants to help him as he grows.
	God loves him and wants him to love God.
	God made the universe and all in it.
	God wants him to pray each day.
	God always answers prayers with "Yes," "No," or "Wait."
	God loves people all over the world.
	God the Holy Spirit is a person who is spirit.
	When he accepts Jesus as His Saviour, the Holy Spirit comes into his life.
About Jesus	Jesus is the Son of God, the Saviour.
	Jesus died on the cross for sin.
	Jesus can give salvation to those who ask.
	Jesus can forgive sin.

| | Jesus loves him even when he sins. |
| | Jesus wants him to be a disciple and follow Him. |

About the Bible
The Bible is an exciting Book to read.
The Bible is a true Book, not fiction.
The Bible is God's Word.
The Bible should be read each day.
The Bible has many important verses to be memorized.
The Bible is God's truth.
The Bible tells what God wants us to know.

About home and parents
Parents have rules for him to follow, but they also have God's rules to follow.
Parents are to the child what God is to the parents.
Parents want him to be a part of the family group.
Home is a secure place where he can find his strength.
Home is a happy place.
Home is a place where he can talk over his problems with his parents.
Home is a place where he can learn to follow rules.

About church and Sunday school
Church is like a school, except that he learns about God and the Bible.
Church is a place where he can worship God.
Church is a place to sing about God.
Church is a place for families.
Church is a happy place where he wants to go.
Church needs his help to be all that it should.

About others
Others include a wider world, far beyond the community.
Others include foreign boys and girls across the sea.
Others need help, which he can give.
Others need the gospel, which he can share.
Others need his prayers.
Others need his money, which he can give.

About angels and last things
Satan is a beautiful angel who sinned against God.
Satan is the most wicked of all created beings.
Satan tempts Christians and leads them astray.
Good angels protect God's people.
Good angels are God's messengers to men and carry out God's judgments.

Heaven is for those who have accepted Christ as their personal Saviour.

People who do not accept Christ as their Saviour will be separated from God forever.

WHAT A CHILD OF TEN AND ELEVEN CAN LEARN

About God	God is Spirit, who is everywhere, but whose home is in heaven.
	God is all powerful, but He permits evil things to happen.
	God is all wise, but He permits men to choose between Him and sin, even though He knows what is best.
	God is one, but He is a triune being: Father, Son (Jesus Christ), and Holy Spirit.
	God is absolutely perfect, holy, and just.
	God hates all sin.
	God cares for and protects His children.
	God wants to show him His will for his life.
About Jesus	Jesus took on Himself the body of a man so He could do what God had planned.
	Jesus fulfilled part of God's great plan for the child, to bring him to God; the child must fulfill the other, to accept what Jesus did on the cross.
	Jesus shows him how to live for God, for His perfect life is a pattern for all.
	Jesus took the punishment for the sins of all people on Himself at Calvary.
	Jesus became alive again and lives in heaven.
	Jesus Christ was born of a virgin.
About the Bible	The Bible has the answers to all his everyday problems.
	The Bible can help him live a happy life.
	The Bible tells the history of God's work among men.
	The Bible is God's Word, the authority for life.
	The Bible is set in the culture of another kind of people. He needs to understand that culture to understand the Bible.

The Bible is without error.

The Holy Spirit guided the writers of the Bible books.

The Bible is a Book to honor and to memorize. It is God's truth to put into everyday practice.

The Bible is God's truth for all men. He needs to share it with others.

The Bible, which is God's Word, is to be obeyed.

About home and parents

The home and parents are part of God's plan for him.

The home and parents function as part of God's plan, but he should do his part too.

He should show loyalty to his home and parents.

He should show honor to his home and parents.

He should accept correction from his parents, for this will help him become a strong leader.

He should begin to see what makes a Christian home, looking toward the day when he will start one.

About church and Sunday school

The church is a fellowship of believers in Christ.

The church brings him in contact with Christian leaders.

The church trains him in worship, study, prayer, witness, service, and fellowship.

The church is a place where he can serve God.

The church is a place where he can learn to practice Christian giving and outreach.

He can learn about the ordinances.

About others

Others need his respect for their thoughts, their possessions, their rights.

Others need his understanding.

Others need his help.

He must show others honesty, loyalty, and fair play.

Others need his forgiveness.

Others need his prayers.

Others fit into God's plans, just as he does.

About angels and last things

Satan is the ruler of spiritual wickedness.

Satan wants to keep people from coming to God.

God has a plan for the future, which will come to pass.

People who have trusted Christ as their Saviour and have died will be raised from the dead when Christ returns.

Satan and his angels will be cast into the lake of fire for eternal punishment.

People who have not trusted Christ as their Saviour will spend eternity in hell.

Index

A

Afterlife, supposed, 58
Approach:
    realism, 17, 18
    simplicity, 17-18

B

Belief:
    John on, 83
    nature of, 86-87
    reasons for in child, 83
Bibles for children:
    confusion of child, 124
    frustration of child, 124
    rebellion of child, 124-25
    simpler versions, 125
    versions for child, 5
Blasphemy, 136
Body as temple, 39
"Born again," Paul on, 24

C

Children:
    asking questions of, 18
    education of:
        humor of God, 3
        nature hikes, 3
        rocks, 4
        for toddlers, 3
    learning by age:
        2-3, 142-43
        4-5, 143-44
        6-7, 144-46
        8-9, 146-48
        10-11, 148-50
    questions for:
        adoption by God, 139
        belief in Bible, 135
        big bang, 139
        blasphemy, 136
        careless words, 136-37
        Christian, nature of, 134

Children (*cont.*)
    church, attendance of, 135
    commands of God, obedience to, 134
    eternity, 140
    evolution, 139
    God as spirit, 133
    heaven, 137
    and Holy Spirit, 136
    Jesus, return of, 139-40
    Jesus today, 137
    knowledge of by God, 136
    love of God, 135
    punishment from God, 135
    Satan, nature of, 138-39
    sin, 135-36
    skeptics, 137
    Sunday school, 134-35
    temptation, 137-38
    unanswered prayers, 138
  truths found by, 25-26
    basic beliefs, 26
    early school, 25-26
Christ, Jesus:
  and Adam and Eve fantasy about, 43-44
  after Resurrection:
    and Apostles, instructions to, 74-75
    appearances of, 74
    ascension of, 75
    final appearance, 75
    and young people, teaching of, 75-76
  and afterlife, supposed, 58
  birth, fairy story from Luke about, 47-48
  child, reactions of to, 50-51
  childhood of, 51-52
  "Christmas story," 47
  coming to save, 83-84
    John on, 84
    personal nature of God, 84
  compassion of, 55-58
    grief, and Mary, 55, 56
    Lazarus, imaginary raising of, 56
    and Luke, verses of, 55
    weeping of, 56, 57
  demons, delusions about, 59
  epilepsy, fantasized curing of, 59
  "evil," expulsion of, 59-60
  "evil," nonsense about, 44
  and foot washing, 55
  giving life to in teaching, 87

  as healer, fantasy about, 58-59
  and Herod, 50
  humanness of, 52-53
  and Joseph, actual father of, 47-48
  Mary, supposed reactions of to imaginary angel, 45-46
  prophecy about, alleged, 43
  reasons for coming, 81-82
    and child, 82
    and "Fall" of man, 81
    and human nature, 82
    and Satan, 81, 82
    sin, punishment of, 82
  reasons for death:
    and Fall of man, 64
    Corinthians on, 64
    Paul on, 64
    redemption from of, 64-65
    repentance, 65
    and Satan's power, 64
    Scriptures on, 64, 65
  and Satan, imaginary figure, 44
  Scriptures for discussion of, 87-89
  as servant, 53-55
    attributes of servant, 54
  sharing of, 80-81
    and children, 80-81
    right method of, 80
  shepherds, 48-49
  virgin birth:
    denial of, 44-45
    Luke on, 45
    Matthew on, 45-46
  wise men, 49-50
Confession, 85-86
  for child, 86
  reasons for, 85
Cross, death of Jesus on:
  acceptance of sacrifice by man, 69
  child, "information" for, 67
  pain of, 66
  and Satan, 66
    defeat of, 66-67
  summary, 90
  willingness of Christ to take, 67-68
Crucifixion. *See* Cross

D

Daily life, 27-28
  and adult, 27
  and child, 28
David, psalm by, 24

E

Epilepsy, medieval delusion about, 59
Eternity:
    of God, 8-9
    nature, 84
    to child, 140
Evil:
    and darkness, 14-15
    and Satan, 15
Evolution, 139

F

Faith:
    acceptance, 79
    in children, 79, 80
    and creation, material, 79
    and family, 123-24
    God, constancy of, 78
    growth of, 124
    and love, 130
    nature, 78-79
    points to remember, 77
    unseen, 78-79
Fall, of Man, 64, 81
Forgiveness, 61-62
    child, ideas of, 62
    and perfection of Christ, 62

G

Garden of Eden, 43-45
Gifts, personal:
    artist, 102
    handiwork, 103
        needlepoint, 103
        quilts, 103
    literature, 105-06
        poems, 105
        stories, 105
    music, 104
        author, daughter of, 104
        David, King, 104
        hymns, 104
    nature, 101-02
    photography, 102-03
        example, 103
    science, 105
    talents, nature of, 102
    woodworking, 104
Gifts, spiritual, 106-08
    and Christ, 107
    Corinthians on, 106

James on, 106
    nature, 107
    Peter on, 107
    Scriptures on, 107-08
    use, 107
God:
    answers to child about, 9-10
    attitudes to of creation, 24
    authority of, 14
    Bible stories, 7
    description of in Bible:
        for child, 19
        as creator, 21-22
        justice of, 19-20
        and Psalms, 19
        punishment from ,20-21
    eternity of, 8-9
    identify of, 12-13
    infinitude of, 8
    Isaiah on, 9-10
    John on, 9
    making personal to child, 5-6
    nature, 10-11
    omnipresence of, 16-17
    omniscience of, 16-17
    origin of, 8-9
    plans of for Man, 25
    and science, 11
    surveillance by, 11
    as unexplainable, 8-9

H

Happiness, lack of by man, 82-83
Heaven, 137
Holy Spirit:
    to child, 93-97
    connection of to Christ, 92
    enlightenment from, 96-97
    functions, 91-92
    as guide, 92, 94, 95-96
    as helper, 93-94
    intercession by, 92
    John on, 93
    in life, 92
    reasons for, 95
    renewal, 97
    Scriptures about, 97-100
    sealing in faith, 99-100
    as spiritual teacher, 94-95

J

Jesus: *See* Christ, Jesus

L

Love:
  and acceptance of Jesus, 127
  action of, 129
  and Apostles, 126
  in child, 128
  Corinthians on, 130
  Ephesians on, 131
  and faith, 130
  giving of, 130
  and God, 15-16, 127
    for all, 15
    location of, 15
    rejection of, 16
    spreading, 15-16
  and Jesus' death, 128
  Jesus on, 129-30
  and life stage, 141-42
  nature, 126
  and people, 126-27
  Peter on, 131
  and salvation, 128-29
  and Satan, 129
  sharing, 127
  source of, 127
  summary, 108

M

Man, dominion of, 24

P

Parents:
  bonding of children to, 2
  discussing God with children, 1
  as examples, 2
Peer pressure, 28
Pilate, Pontius, 70-71
  and Barabas, 71
  cowardice of, 71
Prayer:
  for adult, 110-11
  asking for things, 121-22
  and children, 89, 111, 114, 118-19,
    122
    example, 89
  daily, 118
  example of, 112-114
  functions of, 109-10, 117-18
  and God, 111, 112
  importance of, 112
  intercession, 112

  and Jesus, 114-15
  and life, 119
  Matthew on, 115-16
  points to remember, 115-16
  privacy for, 115
  need for, 111
  questions for children, 122
  Scriptures on, 116-17, 119-21

R

Repentance, 84-85
Resurrection:
  bone-breaking, absence of, 72
  burial, 72-73
  and child, 73-74
  and Joseph of Arimathea, 72
  and Mary Magdalene, 73
  Matthew on, 73
  and Nicodemus, 72
  prophecies about, 72-73
  removal from cross, 72
  soldiers, 72
Right vs. wrong, knowledge of, 28

S

Satan:
  vs. Christ, 66-67
  vs. love, 129
  nature of, 138-39
  power of, 64
Second Coming, 139-40
Sin:
  and child, 63
  and drift away from God, 63
  forgiveness of, 90
  power and nature of, 62-63
  punishment of, 82
  questions about, 135-36
Scripture on, 62, 63
Skeptics:
  and children, 40
  and Holy Spirit as helper, 40, 41

T

Ten Commandments:
  adultery, 31
  and centering on God, 33
  coveting neighbor's effects, 32
  discussion with children, 32-33
  false testimony, 31-32

God, primacy of, 28-29
  idols, ban on, 29
  Jesus on, 33
  misuse of name, 29
  murder, 30-31
  parents, honoring of, 30
  sabbath, 29-30
  sacrifice by parents for children, 30
  theft, 31
Trial of Christ, as degradation ritual:
  and Caiaphas, 69-70
  and Judas Iscariot, 69
  truth, discussion of by Christ, 70

Trinity:
  components, 36
  Father, 36-37
  Holy Spirit, 38-39, 40
  human analogy, 41-42
  Jesus as Son, 36, 37
  obedience to, 37-39
  sin, forgiveness of, 36-37

V

Virgin birth, *See* Christ